COME ALIVE:

Conversations with Scripture

This book came to life over the span of 90 very early morning prayer and prompting sessions. I couldn't have done any of them without a partner in the hilarity of empty-nest living, my wife Julie.

Much gratitude also goes to the many hundreds of people who have re-ordered their lives around engaging with the Word before entering the world. You, too, have helped Scripture come alive in our communities.

Introduction
Scripture Comes Alive

On many occasions in my time in pastoral ministry, I have recommended to people that they *"read the Bible"* as part of their life with God. Sometimes, in exasperation, I felt like grabbing them by the shoulders, giving a good shake, and imploring, *"Just read the Bible, will ya?!"*

Except now I know that I was doing little more than giving a tone-deaf lecture to the Ethiopian eunuch in Acts 8:31, who asks plaintively, *"How can I . . . unless someone explains it to me?"*

That realization formed the genesis of this reading guide through the Gospel of Matthew. Whether it's at the church I serve, Good Shepherd Church in Charlotte, North Carolina, or people following online or reading this book, I have stopped demanding—*"Read more!"*—and started empowering—*"Here are ways to understand what we're reading together."* I no longer want to cajole people into reading the Bible; I want to come alongside and give just enough insight to people so they can understand and delight in the Scripture they do read.

As we enter Matthew's world, I come to this joyful task with five core convictions:

1. **The Bible is not a book; it's a library.** I cringe when I hear Scripture called "the Good Book," but I come alive when it's named "the Great Library." The biblical library contains sixty-six books written by as many as forty authors over a time span of more than 1,000 years and in multiple writing styles. Within the biblical library, we have historical narrative, legal directives, songs of faith, words of wisdom, letters from prison to churches in crisis, and in terms of our present study, an entirely new genre called *Gospel,*

biography for the purpose of proclamation. Four inspired biographies with one inspiring subject: Jesus.

2. As I heard in seminary, **Context Is Everything (C.I.E.).** *Context* here has at least two meanings. First, we explore the literary context within Matthew's Gospel itself. We can understand what Matthew says in one part of his Gospel only when we first understand its overall thrust. Even more deeply, we best understand one section within Matthew when we understand those sections that come before it and after it. Second, in addition to the literary context within the Gospel, we also understand that the cultural, geographical, and historical context of Matthew's own life and world play a tremendously important role in shaping his book. As far as we can, we'll seek to understand the role of place, time, and values in Matthew's hands as he tells the story of Jesus.

3. **Reading *the Bible* is much more interesting than reading *Bible verses*.** Matthew is not a mere collection of isolated sayings or spectacular events. It is, instead, an intricate whole with a purposeful design, the product of a literary and theological genius named Matthew. We'll spend less time memorizing snapshots and more time understanding the narrative flow.

4. **When people ask, "Do you interpret the Bible *literally* or *symbolically*?" the correct answer is *literarily*.** When we understand that it is a library and not a book (see #1 above), we realize that the first task of any interpreter is to determine the genre of a particular book, or even section within a book, and then understand it accordingly. It's why the interpretive task for the book of Revelation is much different than for Proverbs. In terms of Matthew, there are many moments that are literal, a few that are symbolic, a few more that are subtly comedic, and others that are a combination of all of the above. We'll be interpreting this Gospel literarily.

5. ***God-breathed* is more alive than *God-dictated* ever could be.** We believe with St. Paul that "all Scripture is God-breathed" (2 Tim. 3:16). What does that mean, and how is it different from God-dictated? Well, if the Bible were God-dictated, the authors would be little more than scribes with no more creativity than robots. God said it, they transcribed it, and we believe it. God-breathed is so much different, more alive, and warmer than that. God-breathed means that God took the personalities of the biblical authors and breathed life and truth into their words without diminishing who they were as men and women. It's why you see so much of Paul's personality, complete with quirks and eccentricities, in his letters to the New Testament churches. It's why you see the thunder of Peter in his letters, the art of David in his songs, and even the despair of Solomon in Ecclesiastes. For the purposes of this study, then, I am so grateful that God used the personality of Matthew to help us gaze on the person of Jesus. After all, isn't gazing on the person of Jesus the ultimate goal for any of us who dare to open Scripture?

With those convictions and that understanding, get ready for a ninety-day journey through the Gospel of Matthew. We're not speed-reading through the Word of God; we're savoring a small morsel each day, knowing that we'll be different at the end of our trek than we were at its beginning.

Day One
Introduction to Matthew

....

Today, as we begin at the beginning, take a breath. A deep one. Pause. Admit to God that the biblical world you're about to enter is very different from your own in terms of geography, customs, and assumptions. Now invite God to bring clarity to your mind and eagerness to your heart as we start ninety days together. Good. Let's start.

How to Begin?

How can we begin this beginning Gospel? How can we bridge the great distance in time, values, and culture between Matthew's world and ours? Maybe more than anything, how can we ensure that our encounter with this Gospel moves from mere words on a page to the Spirit invading our heart? Well, the answers to those questions begin with addressing these: Who was Matthew? What was his Gospel? When did he write? And ultimately, why did he take the time and make the effort to compose this story?

Who?

Matthew is wonderfully sly in placing himself within Jesus' story. We learn in Matthew 9:9 that our author was a tax collector for the Romans—which makes him a traitor to his own people—before Jesus called him to be one of the Twelve. Upon that call, Matthew left his previous life behind but took his pen with him and became a masterful recorder and reporter of all that Jesus said and did. Think of the contrast embedded within Matthew's very person: a Roman citizen and so highly educated; yet also Hebrew born and bred and so adept at keeping records. As the story begins, he must have been a man at odds with himself: Jew, yet traitor; Roman, yet outsider; disciple, yet so vulnerable to forgetting the same faith that defined him. The transformation of the characters in the book must mimic that which happened in the author himself.

What?

Well, what is a *Gospel*? As many of you know, *gospel* means "good news," and the four New Testament accounts of Jesus' life are certainly that. Yet there's more, as the Gospels comprise their own unique literary form. If they're *biography*, they're frustratingly slim on details that interest us: *"What did Jesus look like?" "What were his early years like?" "Who were his heroes?" "Did he fight with his brothers?" "What kind of report cards did he get?"* The Gospels are silent on all those matters. If they are merely *proclamation*, they give us a great deal of narrative before leaving us with a message. What shall we say then? A working definition is this: the four Gospels are biographical sketches written for the purpose of proclamation leading to decision.

With that mostly settled, what sets Matthew's Gospel apart? How is it similar to and different from its three first cousins? Matthew's Gospel follows much the same story line as Mark's. (Luke has significant distinction from Matthew and Mark, while John is a different animal altogether.) So, the question remains: Is Matthew a version of Mark on steroids, or is Mark a *Reader's Digest* condensed version of Matthew? No certain answer exists, though most experts believe that Mark was written first, and Matthew had access to that material and added more *meat* to the *skin and bones* of Mark. What type of *meat* does Matthew add that Mark omits? A casual look at a "Red Letter" Bible—one that prints Jesus' words in red in contrast to the rest of the text in black—will quickly answer this question. In Matthew, Jesus is a man of words, while in Mark, he is a man of action. For example, Matthew's version contains the "Sermon on the

Mount"—three straight chapters of solid red (Matthew 5–7)—while Mark's has no such sermon at all.

Finally, a word about how this Gospel functioned with its original audience. Like all biblical books, Matthew was *not* written to be read; it was composed to be *heard*. Matthew writes for the ear and not the eye. Why is this so? Because the majority of people in ancient Israel were illiterate; when they gathered as the church, the few educated ones among them would read the text publicly. This is why Paul says "faith comes from hearing" (Rom. 10:17) when many of us might think it comes by reading. To get the most out of many sections of Matthew, you'll want to experience them as his first audience did. In your case, it will come by reading passages out loud, even to yourself.

When?

The Gospel of Matthew was likely written between AD 50 and 70, within fifteen or twenty years of the events it describes. We know the early church told and retold and re-retold the stories of Jesus to itself. We also know the church equipped its people through letters that were both corrective (1 Corinthians) and instructive (James). We further know from 1 Thessalonians 4 that as the early church dealt with death among its ranks—some due to martyrdom and others because of natural causes—these first believers wanted to ensure that a permanent record existed of Jesus' life and the responses to it. Finally, in God's wisdom, Matthew is one of the men selected to collect the dots of Jesus' life and teaching so the church could later connect those same dots in the Gospel.

Why?

Each Gospel has a slightly different twist and purpose. Together they form a micro-library, the Bible's unique biography section, within the larger biblical library, and the four give us a much fuller, more compelling picture of Jesus and his first followers than any single volume could. From the beginning, Matthew sets out to demonstrate that Jesus is the fulfillment of the story of Israel, the King of the Jews, the arrival of the much-anticipated Messiah. Matthew's audience is made up primarily of followers of Jesus who are of Jewish descent. Matthew pays attention to Jewish customs and scriptures in a way that John, for example, would not. The Gospel authors use different strategies to reach different audiences. This is not cause for alarm but for celebration, as it underscores that the Bible is inspired, eternal, and true in ways that thrill us and mold us.

Day Two
Matthew 1:1–17

M atthew reveals his purpose in his very first sentence: "This is the genealogy of Jesus the Messiah the son of David, the son of Abraham." Jesus wasn't literally David's son, and David wasn't literally Abraham's son. Yet Jesus is in the line of both ancestors and completes their standing as representative of Israel: Abraham as the *father* of the nation and David as its ideal king.

Now, why in the world would anyone start a biography with a genealogy? If storytellers need to grab their audience's attention from the opening words, why this sleep-inducing list of names and begats? Why begin with an extended trip through Jesus' family graveyard?

To answer that, you have to remember that you are not Matthew's intended audience. His Gospel was written to first-century Jews, and it was graciously preserved for you. His audience would have been mesmerized with this genealogy, as they would have heard the names of some of the most famous figures in the history of Israel. Remember as well that this book wasn't written to be read but to be heard; Matthew crafts his words together so they have maximum aural punch.

Two items of particular note in this genealogy give us important information about Jesus' identity:

1.   By tracing Jesus' ancestry through Abraham, Matthew underscores how the Messiah fulfills everything God ever intended for Israel. When Luke writes Jesus' genealogy, he traces his lineage of Jesus through Adam, reinforcing his contention that Jesus is the Savior of all people.

2.   Matthew goes to great lengths to include people in Jesus' family tree that most of his contemporaries would have preferred to leave out. First, he includes four women,

and that fact alone goes against the customary "ancestry. com" of the ancient world. At each mention of the women involved, the listening audience would have raised their eyebrows and perked their ears: "He included her? And her?" Look at Matthew 1:3: "Judah the father of Perez and Zerah, whose mother was Tamar." The sordid tale of Tamar's impregnation at the hands of her father-in-law, Judah, is in Genesis 38, and—miracle of miracles—she is the heroine of the story!

Then in verse 5, we read: "Salmon the father of Boaz, whose mother was Rahab." What is Rahab's *nickname*? Rahab the harlot. That's right. A prostitute is part of the genealogy of the Messiah. At the beginning, Matthew lets us know that nothing in your background or on your résumé disqualifies you for a role in kingdom significance. The next part of verse 5 reads as follows: "Boaz the father of Obed, whose mother was Ruth." This is the same Ruth, of course, who has an Old Testament book named after her. And she is a Moabitess: an outsider, a foreigner, a stranger. She, too, has a place in the Messiah's family tree. And finally in verse 6: "David was the father of Solomon, whose mother had been Uriah's wife." In other words, Bathsheba. She is the victim of David's whims. Uriah is the victim of David's power. Yet God massages something good out of that adulterous and murderous beginning. So, while the genealogy highlights many of Israel's heroes, it also spotlights some of its warts . . . and that's precisely the point. Our Messiah is here to redeem.

From the beginning, then, Matthew tells, not just history, but history with a purpose: Jesus fulfills every hope of Israel and is its eternal king.

From the beginning, the Gospel brings outsiders in. That includes you, for this Gospel is the story of not just Israel's king but your Messiah.

Day Three
Matthew 1:18-25

....

Many of us know this story, but we haven't really read this story. Today, we will not only read the story, but we will investigate how much of the Christmas story comes from Luke as opposed to Matthew.

Notice how purposeful Matthew is at the outset: "This is how the birth of Jesus the Messiah came about" (1:18). The unveiling of Jesus is no spur-of-the-moment action by God; instead, it is the culmination of a rescue plan for the human race that predates creation itself. It is vital for Matthew to demonstrate to his largely Jewish audience that the story he tells is the story of their own fulfillment in the life of Jesus, the awaited Messiah.

Because Matthew's audience is Jewish, they would have understood some things about the language and cultural innuendo that perplex us, such as, how can Joseph wish to "divorce" Mary when she is not yet his wife (v. 19)? In ancient Jewish life, a marriage had three phases: (1) the engagement or marriage contract, which was arranged by the parents of the man and woman, often from the time of childhood (marriage was too important to be left to the whims of the human heart); (2) the betrothal, a one-year period of waiting that commenced as soon as the couple *ratified* the earlier decision of the parents; and (3) the marriage itself. The betrothal was as binding as the marriage, though the couple did not consummate it physically through the sexual act. That was reserved for the wedding night.

This is why we read that Joseph wants to "divorce" his fiancée! It sounds a bit bewildering to us, but it was common sense to them. Notice that in verse 20 an "angel of the Lord appeared to [Joseph] in a dream." Get used to that method of communication, as we will see it a great deal over the next couple of chapters.

Next: "[W]hat is conceived in her is from the Holy Spirit" (v. 20), Matthew tells us. In Jewish thought, the Holy Spirit brings the truth of God into the hearts of human beings and empowers us to understand truth when we see it.

In this case, in Matthew, the Spirit will teach us something about the role of Messiah: "You are to give him the name Jesus, because he will save the people from their sins" (v. 21) *Jesus* is the Greek pronunciation of *Joshua* or *Yeshua*, which means "the Lord saves." I find it fascinating that Jesus does not come primarily to show us a new way to live or to help us reach our full potential or even to make us feel good about ourselves. That's how we have made him into our image. No, he came to solve our greatest need, which is forgiveness from sin. We're not *mistakers* who need correction; we're *sinners* who need salvation.

Matthew 1:22–23 shows Matthew's essence as both author and Jew, dropping hints on a theme that will dominate upcoming sections: Jesus' entrance into planet Earth is part of a much larger and much longer plan designed to complete the mission given to Israel in Genesis 12. Here's what it says: "All this took place to fulfill what the Lord had said through the prophet: 'The virgin will conceive and give birth to a son, and they will call him Immanuel' (which means 'God with us.')." Matthew reminds us that this birth is neither accidental nor incidental, as the prophet to whom he refers is Isaiah, writing many hundreds of years before Mary was pregnant or Jesus was born. Why the distinction between *Immanuel* and *Jesus*? There was no conflict in either Matthew's mind or Joseph's; *Immanuel* is who Jesus is (God with us) and *Jesus* is what Jesus does (saves people from their sins).

In Matthew's telling, the actual birth of Jesus occurs mostly offstage, as we don't get any of the birth details that most interest us as modern people. Instead, the brevity of detail contributes to the gravity of the topic: "But he did not consummate their marriage until she gave birth to a son. And he gave him the name Jesus" (v. 25).

In contrast to the brevity of Matthew's nativity narrative, Luke is the source of many of the best-known pieces of the Christmas story. His Gospel is where we read about the in utero leap of John the Baptist when his mother, Elizabeth, meets pregnant Mary. Luke alone records the lengthy conversations between Mary and the angel Gabriel. The trip to Bethlehem, where there is "no room in the inn," swaddling clothes, and "they laid him in a manger?" Luke, Luke, and more Luke. What about the interaction between the terrified shepherds and the comforting angels? You got it: Luke yet again. No doubt your most vivid Christmas memories find their source in the way Dr. Luke tells it. All that is why the climactic scene of *A Charlie Brown's Christmas* is Linus's recitation of Luke 2:1–21 and not Matthew 1:18–25.

The one story that Matthew includes, which we don't find in Luke? The visit of the Magi. And that's where we will turn next as we read Matthew 2:1–12.

....

We're not* mistakers *who need correction; we're* sinners *who need salvation, and that's the story Matthew weaves for us.

....

Day Four
Matthew 2:1-12

....

Today, once again, we get to dig into a story virtually all of us have heard but few of us have studied: the visit of the Magi to baby Jesus. While "We Three Kings" may be a fine hymn, it is hardly based on biblical text!

The first difference between the Magi story of folklore and that which we find in the Bible is found in 2:1 and the reference to Jerusalem. Wait—what? The Magi went to Jerusalem first? That star wasn't hanging right over the manger in Bethlehem?! No, it wasn't. They came to Jerusalem first, because this story is less about gifts for baby Jesus and more about what happens when a king is born in a land that already has a king.

Who were these "Magi from the east"? Not kings. More likely philosophers, astronomers, or spiritual advisers. Most certainly they were pagan, not Jews from Israel but idol worshipers from points east of Israel, either Babylon or Persia. And yet look at their question in verse 2, in which they unknowingly reveal the purpose of this particular Gospel: "Where is the one who has been born king of the Jews?"

The reaction of King Herod—the sitting king in a land where a king was just born—is priceless: "When King Herod heard this he was disturbed, and all Jerusalem with him" (v. 3). Remember: Herod is a representative of the Roman Empire, the occupying force in Israel. Why is all of Jerusalem "disturbed" with him? Because the people know from experience that if Herod's not happy, no one will be happy.

In verse 4, therefore, Herod calls together the religious leadership of the Jews to find out where the Messiah is to be born. The priests and teachers point to Micah 5:2, 4, which Matthew then quotes, providing continuing evidence to his readers that the "Jesus Rescue Plan" has been in the works for hundreds of years.

Armed with this knowledge, Herod devises a deceptive plan in which he lets the Magi know to look in Bethlehem and asks a small favor: "As soon as you find him, report to me, so that I too may go and worship him" (Matt. 2:8). It isn't difficult to discern Herod's true agenda. Given his track record, it's clear that his intent is infant assassination and not Savior adoration.

The Magi then follow the king's order and the star's direction (v. 9) and find the baby in Bethlehem. This is the part of the story we know from folklore, missing all the political and religious intrigue that preceded it. The Magi enter the house and bow down to worship the true king. Their gifts reveal much about not only the magi but the destiny of this child: gold is for a king, frankincense is for a priest, and myrrh is for one who is to die (myrrh passed for embalming fluid in ancient times). While not exactly popular at a modern baby shower, these gifts are essential to the purpose of this newborn king, who will ascend to royal splendor in the most unexpected ways at the end of the Gospel.

Note the end of this scene: "Having been warned in a dream not to go back to Herod, they [the Magi] returned to their country by another route" (v. 12). There's that dream communication again, and more of it appears in our next passage of Scripture.

The earthly king is relentless in his efforts to destroy heaven's royalty. But God will always have the last word, as nothing will stop the unfolding of the Messiah's reign. Even if he has to sojourn in Egypt to survive, just like his ancestors before him, he will prevail.

Jesus' reign is sure, even when the obstacles are high and the situation is bleak.

Day Five
Matthew 2:13-23

···

Today, you'll get to see some patterns of great significance in the reading of Scripture in general and something of major importance in the message of Matthew in particular.

Repetition is the Bible's "neon light." Writing was hard work in the first century. Materials were expensive; labor was intensive. Therefore, you can take for granted that if an inspired author goes to the trouble of repeating something, you are meant to notice it! In addition, the mechanics of *publishing* in those days did not allow for boldface, ALL CAPS, or headings. Repetition was the major tool in the arsenal of any writer.

In today's section, we'll see three major repetitions: (1) "warned in a dream"; (2) "Get up / got up" and (3) "fulfilled." Whatever we're supposed to glean from this slice of Matthew, it revolves around these recurrences.

In Matthew 2:13–15, we see all three recurring themes in just a few verses. After the Magi leave the little family of Mary, Joseph, and Jesus, an angel warns Joseph "in a dream" to "get up" and take his wife and baby to Egypt. Why? Herod is the king in a land where a king has just been born, and Herod wants to take the newborn king out. He becomes fixated on erasing Jesus.

Joseph obeys: "So he got up." I love the simplicity of that: he was told to get up . . . and he got up. God's command yields obedience. This is the Lord's way of saying I won't do *for* you what I need to do *with* you.

What was the purpose of the sojourn in Egypt? Not only to preserve Jesus' life but to fulfill the words of Hosea 11:1: "Out of Egypt I called my son." In a deeper sense, why must Jesus come "out of Egypt"? Well, what did the nation of Israel do? They came out of

Egypt in the exodus! Jesus is fulfilling and completing everything that is Israel, and Matthew wants to make sure his largely Jewish readership knows that.

Matthew 2:16–18 is known as "the Massacre of the Innocents." Herod does what psychopaths do when they don't get their way; they make other people pay for their own insecurities. How many Bethlehem boys died in this monstrosity? It was a relatively small village, so experts suggest no more than thirty or so. Reading that number, you may at first be relieved . . . "Oh, not thousands" . . . . unless one of the thirty belonged to someone you know. It goes to show the degree to which the leaders of our world attempt to rebuke the reign of God. Notice as well that even this sad moment was foreshadowed in the Hebrew Scripture: "Then what was said through the prophet Jeremiah was fulfilled . . ." (vv. 17–18).

Ultimately, Herod dies, and since Joseph could not read about it in his Twitter feed, he gets the information in Matthew's preferred method: a dream. Notice verses 19–21: "After Herod died, an angel of the Lord appeared in a dream to Joseph in Egypt and said, 'Get up, take the child and his mother and go to the land of Israel, for those who were trying to take the child's life are dead.' So he got up . . ." There it is again! Matthew says to us, "Notice this! Joseph is our get up / got up guy!"

Yet the family's arrival back *home* in Israel doesn't result in complete freedom from danger. Herod has a son, Archelaus, and that son possesses some of the old man's insecurities and rage. So, what happens? You got it! Another dream: "Having been warned in a dream, he withdrew to the district of Galilee, and he went and lived in a town called Nazareth" (vv. 22–23). Why Nazareth? Of course, Matthew has the answer: "So was fulfilled what was said through the prophets, that he would be called a Nazarene" (v. 23).

At every level, the forces of evil are arrayed against the arrival of the king. And yet at every moment, God frustrates his enemies, outwits his opponents, and preserves the Messiah. The reign of Messiah will never be overthrown, and what we now know by faith will one day be within our sight.

Erasing Jesus never works because Jesus never fails.

Day Six
Matthew 3:1-12

E ach of the four Gospel authors pauses the story of Jesus in order to tell the tale of John the Baptist. They make us wait for the lead actor by focusing in on one of the supporting cast. They put Messiah on hold to put his cousin in the spotlight (see Mark 1:3–8; Luke 1:57–80; 3:1–20; John 1:6–8, 29–34).

Matthew devotes today's section of the Gospel (3:1–12) to telling his readers about John's role in Jesus' ministry. Matthew summarizes John's ministry by quoting the Baptist's first words, words we hear before Jesus himself speaks: "Repent, for the kingdom of heaven has come near" (v. 2). Now think of what he doesn't say: "The kingdom is near and y'all are good!" "The Messiah is here, and he's come to tell you 'don't change a thing'!" "My cousin is on the way, and he is here to celebrate and affirm the ways you are being true to yourself!" Instead, it's repent. Turn. Change. Lament. Acknowledge the ways you are living for yourself rather than for God.

John's offensive message continues with the clothes he wears and the food he eats (v. 4), and most especially, how he treats those who come to observe his ministry, even if they are baptized (vv. 7–10). Of course, Matthew has to tell us that all of this is part of the plan that stretches back centuries, foreshadowed in the words of the prophet Isaiah (v. 3). Even this pesky, offensive forerunner of the Messiah is part of God's unfolding plan to fulfill everything about Israel in its new King Jesus.

John's closing words (vv. 11–12) are particularly threatening: "After me comes one who is more powerful than I, whose sandals I am not worthy to carry. . . . His winnowing fork is in his hand, and he will clear his threshing floor, gathering his wheat into the barn after burning up the chaff with unquenchable fire." Reading between

John's lines: "If you think I'm offensive, just wait until you meet my cousin!"

Apparently, our inspired Gospel writers all felt that we needed to hear from offensive John to prepare us to hear from more offensive Jesus. Wow. The real Jesus, the one revealed in the Gospels and revered by the church for millennia, had a rough forerunner in John. That's because Jesus' message is less about affirmation than about transformation. It's offensive before it's redemptive. Grace is insulting before it's amazing.

> **Grace insults before it amazes because you have to admit you're a mess in order to embrace Messiah.**

Day Seven
Matthew 3:13-17

The reading for today is short, but it involves a story that is quite perplexing at first glance: Jesus is baptized by John. For years, many have wondered, "If baptism is for the forgiveness of sins, and Jesus never sinned, why in the world did he get baptized?" It's a vexing question, but one I believe we'll be able to answer today.

Notice how the story begins with a note of geography: "Then Jesus came from Galilee to the Jordan to be baptized by John" (v. 13). This change of scenery appears to be the first step in Jesus' journey into the wilderness.

When Jesus presents himself to John for baptism, John has the reaction we would have: "I need to be baptized by you, and do you come to me?" (v. 14).

Yet Jesus overrides John's attempted veto. His reasoning? "Let it be so now; it is proper for us to do this to fulfill all righteousness" (v. 15). We see yet again how one of Matthew's overriding purposes comes out: "This baptism must happen," Jesus says, "because it is part of the long, unfolding plan of God for me to complete everything that is Israel."

Something else is at work too. Look back at Matthew 3:7, where John's baptizing ministry begins: "But when he saw many of the Pharisees and Sadducees coming to where he was baptizing. . . ." Note: they were not coming to be baptized but only to *investigate* baptism. In general, the righteous, religious Jews were not submitting themselves to John's baptism; that was reserved for the great unwashed, both unrighteous Jews and converts from paganism. So Jesus' submission to John is less about his own sin (of which there was none) and more about his radical invitation to all, Jew and Gentile, sinner and saint, put-together and falling-apart.

With that rationale, John consents to the baptism, Jesus enters the waters of the Jordan, presumably gets "dunked," and then emerges out of the water. That's when things get even more interesting. Heaven opens, and Jesus sees the Spirit of God descend on him. Did others see it? We're not sure, because Matthew does not say. Then a voice from heaven declares, "This is my Son, whom I love; with him I am well pleased" (v. 17). That line combines Psalm 2:7, a song that faithful Jews knew applied to Messiah, and Isaiah 42:1, which begins a lengthy description of the "Suffering Servant." Yet again, Jesus in Matthew's hands points to his own appearance and the ministry that ensues as one more piece in God's unfolding plan of redemption.

In that sense, Jesus' baptism is his inauguration into public ministry. The Father announces his Son, Messiah, and here at the beginning suggests that Messiah's route will not be one of ease and comfort but of suffering and sacrifice. The specter of the cross is never far from the Father's mind or Jesus' mission.

Jesus' baptism launched his public ministry. How has your baptism propelled you into ministry?

Day Eight
Matthew 4:1-17

As we left off yesterday's reading, Jesus had been baptized, affirmed, and inaugurated into his public ministry. But there is one more rite of passage he must fulfill in order to live into his identity as the completion of all that is Israel: to be "led by the Spirit into the wilderness to be tempted by the devil" (4:1). Isn't that interesting? The Spirit leads him into a time of testing. This brief story is less a tale of Satan tempting than it is about Spirit-forming. In all that follows, there is never a hint that this is a battle of equals; in his sovereignty, Jesus allows himself to be tested in the region known as the *wilderness*.

And where was that? The wilderness of ancient Palestine was just to the east of Jerusalem and along the Dead Sea. As we continually remember that Jesus completes all that was Israel, remember how the Jews themselves spent forty years wandering? And where? In the wilderness, the Sinai desert. When? Immediately after coming through the waters of the Red Sea. In the same way, Jesus' wilderness experience follows immediately after emerging from the waters of baptism. Matthew wants us to know: This is the newer, better Moses.

After forty days of fasting, "he was hungry" (v. 2). You think? That's when the tempter approaches him—we do not know in what form—and offers a series of three tests:

1. "Tell these stones to become bread." (v. 3)

2. "Throw yourself down [from the top of the temple]." (v. 6)

3. "Bow down and worship me" and you can have all the kingdoms of the world. (v. 9)

In each case, Jesus rebukes the enemy by declaring the scriptures. He quotes directly, in succession, from Deuteronomy 8:3; 6:16, 13. What a priceless gift it is to have the Word embedded in your mind, ready to be used as weaponry at a moment's notice. Beyond that, the second and third tests interest me most: the temptation to cause a spectacle ("throw yourself down" from the temple) and to compromise with evil in order to advance a platform ("bow down and worship me" and you can have all the kingdoms of the world!).

If Jesus had succumbed to the *spectacle* test, he would have created the flimsiest of movements: one based on the latest and greatest show. We know from biblical history and church history that any kind of ministry based solely on spectacles produces faith only in the spectacular! That kind of faith is a mile wide and an inch deep. That's not what Jesus is after for us. If Jesus had compromised even just a little by giving in to Satan in order to gain more territory, the consequences would have been catastrophic.

After Jesus completed his wilderness tests, "the devil left him, and angels came and attended him" (v. 11). What did that look like? We don't know because Matthew doesn't tell us. We do know that receiving such tender attention prepared Jesus for what came next: the launching of his public ministry. Notice the rhythm of Jesus' life: solitude followed by activity, rest followed by work, seclusion followed by engagement. Jesus begins his ministry upon hearing that John the Baptist is in jail (for standing up to Herod). Yet look at Matthew's attention to geography in 4:13. Jesus leaves Nazareth—in a sense, closing the door on one season of life—and moves to the town of Capernaum in the region of Galilee.

Why the move? In yet another case of Matthew being Matthew, it's "to fulfill what was said through the prophet Isaiah" (v. 14). None of this is accidental! It's all the unfolding of an ancient plan, even down to the details of geography. Galilee itself was surrounded by Gentiles; that's why Isaiah called it "Galilee of the Gentiles" (v. 15), yet another reminder that although Jesus' mission in Matthew focuses on Israel and the Jews, it will culminate with a movement into Gentile populations and pagan hearts.

I love Jesus' first recorded words, in verse 17: "Repent, for the kingdom of heaven has come near." Think of what Jesus didn't say:

— "Just chill; you're good the way you are."

— "I'm here to boost your self-esteem."

— "I'm OK, you're OK. Let's be true to ourselves."

None of that modern drivel. Instead: Repent. You're a mess, and you need a messiah. His message has never changed. John's uncompromising word had prepared the way for Jesus' unending truth. What kind of reception does this message receive? What kind of people will Jesus encounter in Galilee? That's for the rest of Matthew 4 . . . tomorrow.

We rarely fall into disaster. Instead, we creep there one compromise at a time. In what area of life are you tolerating compromise with what is most true about you?

Day Nine
Matthew 4:18-25

W hen we left Jesus yesterday, he had just moved out of Nazareth and up to Capernaum, quite likely closing the door on the chapter in his life where his parents supplied him with food and housing. His relocation leads to a new phase in life in another, more prominent way: "As Jesus was walking beside the Sea of Galilee, he saw two brothers, Simon called Peter and his brother Andrew" (4:18).

Who are these men Jesus sees? Simon and Andrew? Why does Jesus target them in his evident search for gospel talent? We don't know because Matthew doesn't say. We do know that Matthew, like Mark, Luke, and John to follow, does not hesitate to share the failures of these men as they follow Jesus. Given that the men called in today's reading became the leaders of leaders in the early church, they clearly do not hide their weaknesses as the church writes its own history. But I'm getting ahead of myself; these guys haven't done anything yet!

Notice the way Jesus calls them: "Come, follow me . . . and I will send you out to fish for people" (v. 19). I will turn you from fishermen to fishers of men. Consider again what Jesus doesn't say in his initial call:

– "Follow me and all your dreams will come true."

– "Follow me and reach your full potential."

– "Follow me and just watch the ladies follow us!"

– "Follow me because we've got a killer band and great children's ministries!"

None of that. He says, "Follow me and I have a project for you." Forgiveness always comes with an assignment. In spite of the abruptness of Jesus' call—and his questionable marketing strategy—he nevertheless bats a thousand! "At once they left their nets and followed him" (v. 20).

In a case of déjà vu all over again, Jesus repeats his personnel recruitment strategy with two more men in verses 21–22. In this case, his targets are "James son of Zebedee and his brother John." There will come a time or two in the ensuing three years where Jesus will no doubt ask himself, "Why did I choose these sons of thunder? And why these pairs of brothers? You know when you mix family and business, trouble is never far away!" The call of James and John is similar to and different from that of Simon and Andrew; it's similar in that the response is instant (Matthew says "immediately"), and different in that James and John leave more behind. Whereas Simon and Andrew "left their nets" (v. 20), James and John "left their boat" as well as their father (v. 22). That suggests that their fishing operation was of a different scale than Simon's and Andrew's; they left not only their livelihood but very likely their legacy as well.

What is the first task of these men who respond so swiftly? Matthew answers this in verses 23–25. Now that Jesus has assembled the first members of his team, he can begin his ministry. It's a mobile ministry that reaches the regions all around Galilee and centers on three activities according to verse 23:

- "teaching in their synagogues": As the subject of his teaching will center on how he is the fulfillment of all that is Israel, of course he goes where the Jews are in order to teach them a new thing.

- "proclaiming the good news of the kingdom": Other translations use the word *preaching*, so we assume Jesus declared truth in a way that engaged both mind and heart.

- "healing every disease and sickness among the people": While his ultimate aim had to do with people's eternal destiny, nevertheless Jesus ministered with compassion to people who were suffering. His ability to heal reveals his authority over both sickness and sin as well as his authority over the human body, a body he designed in the first place.

With his words and actions, Jesus attracts crowds. People arrive from Syria (v. 24) and then from "Galilee, the Decapolis [a federation of "Ten Cities"], Jerusalem, Judea and the region across the Jordan" (v. 25). In this way, Matthew is already dropping a hint as to how his Gospel will conclude, as Jesus' final words in the book are what we refer to as the Great Commission: "Therefore go and make disciples of all nations, baptizing them in the name of the Father and of the Son and of the Holy Spirit, and teaching them to obey everything I have commanded you" (28:19–20). It will start with the children of Israel but inevitably radiate beyond to all lands and to all people.

When church gets it right, it consists of disciples who make more disciples; fishermen who become fishers of men; the *invited* who become the *inviters*. That's a movement to which it is worth saying yes.

"Come, follow me," Jesus says and it turns out that partial acceptance is complete rejection.

Day Ten
Matthew 5:1-12

When we left Jesus yesterday at the end of Matthew 4, he had assembled the inner circle of his Discipleship Team and begun his public ministry. Today we begin what's called "the Sermon on the Mount" (for reasons that will be obvious when we look at Matthew 5:1), a collections of sayings, observations, commands, surprises, and challenges that make up chapters 5–7.

The scope and skill of the Sermon on the Mount bring up a bit of a conundrum. If this is Jesus' masterpiece, why does Luke include only a portion of it in what's called the Sermon on the Plain (Luke 6:20–49) and why do Mark and John not include it at all? Great questions! This is another example of why it is vital to remember that the Bible is not "the Good Book" but it is "the Great Library" and that even within the *biography* section of the library, the four authors have distinct methods, purposes, and objectives. We want to elevate the authority of each and understand that each has a unique way in which God breathed eternity and truth onto, into, and through them.

In this case, we celebrate how God used Matthew's background and personality to breathe out a unique picture of Jesus: the Messiah of the Jews, the fulfillment of everything that was Israel. That includes what we see in 5:1: "Now when Jesus saw the crowds, he went up on a mountainside and sat down. His disciples came to him, and he began to teach them." Well, *who else* in Israel's history had an encounter on a mountain? Right! Moses! Think of the parallels we've seen so far!

- Moses came out of Egypt. So did baby Jesus.

- Moses led people through the water of the Red Sea. Jesus came through the waters of baptism in the Jordan.

- Immediately after the Red Sea parting, Moses and Israel wandered in the wilderness for forty years. Immediately after Jesus was baptized, he wandered in the wilderness and was tempted by the devil for forty days.

- Moses received revelation on Mount Sinai, the Ten Commandments plus more. Jesus gives revelation from the mountainside in Matthew 5–7.

Jesus is the new, better, completed Moses! Matthew is a genius, and Jesus is glorious. How does our glorious Jesus open his sermon? He doesn't offer a canned joke; nor does he promise people that if they listen to the end, he will change their lives. Instead, the beginning is called the *Beatitudes*. Go ahead and read through them now in verses 3–12.

Rather than parse each particular verse, here are a couple of observations. The word "blessed" at the beginning of each beatitude essentially means *happy*. Yet notice: Jesus does not tell us how to be happy. He instead provides nine examples of genuinely happy people: poor in spirit, mourners, meek, righteousness hungry, merciful, pure in heart, peacemakers, persecuted, insulted. When you look at the list that way, you realize quickly, "Those words are not part of any 'how to be happy' podcast I've ever heard!"

In the kingdom that Jesus both reveals and embodies in this Gospel, everything you've thought about life and its meaning and purpose is wrong. Jesus' kingdom is upside down in almost every way: strength comes through weakness, wisdom comes via foolishness, winning arrives through losing, greatness is revealed in serving, and most of all, living comes through dying. It all culminates on the cross and through the resurrection.

The takeaway?

....

Stop trying to be happy. Instead, strive to become godly. You'll get contentment and happiness thrown in, not as the world describes it, but as the Savior defines it.

....

Day Eleven
Matthew 5:13-20

As we left Jesus' "sermon opener" of the Beatitudes, we recognized the upside-down nature of the kingdom and, indeed, of happiness itself. It comes through mourning, meekness, poverty, and persecution. In fact, we can read the entire New Testament through the lens of paradox. Think about it: the first will be last, the greatest will be servant, we find strength in weakness, and at the source of it all is a Savior whose coronation as the king occurs during his execution on a cross. Nothing is as it seems.

Jesus transitions from the paradigm of paradox that opened his sermon into some directed speech in Matthew 5:13: "You are the salt of the earth." Isn't that how we refer to people who are dependable, predictable, and essential? "He's just the salt of the earth," we say of the mechanic down the street or the Sunday school teacher up the road. Yet the way we use the phrase—as fine as it is—is slightly different from Jesus' intention. Remember: he is speaking first to his disciples ("his disciples came to him," 5:1) and second to the assembled crowds. The Sermon on the Mount is almost like a leadership training session in which everyone else gets to listen in.

So, what does the *salt* comparison mean, not only for the crowd in general, but for these leaders-in-training in particular? Well, what did salt do in the ancient world? In a time before refrigeration, it preserved food. It kept it from rot and spoil. In addition, salt then and now brings out the flavor already in the food. It less imposes taste *on* food than lifts out the flavor already *in* it.

How does this apply to those of us walking with Jesus and, even more particularly, those of us in any type of spiritual leadership at all? The gospel is to be preserved, not modernized. It is a treasure to be stewarded and not clay to be molded. We start our mornings in the ancient Word because we will not succumb to "chronological arrogance," thinking that we're the smartest people who've ever lived. No, the gospel of God is not something we invent; it's what we inherit. It's to be preserved.

Those of us in spiritual leadership—whether that's leading a small group, raising children or grandchildren, heading up a ministry team, or even pastoring a church—need to remember that the people in our care already have the "flavor of God" implanted deep within them. We have the enormous privilege of calling that flavor out and empowering people into ministry. It's an old line but still true: a good leader makes you believe in the leader; a great leader makes you believe in yourself. To that, I'd add that a Christian leader makes you believe not just "in yourself" but in Jesus and in the divine gifting that is your birthright by faith.

That idea of impacting the world rather than avoiding it is at the heart of Jesus' next words. He concludes that paragraph with the encouraging promise: "Let your light shine before others, that they may see your good deeds and glorify your Father in heaven" (v. 16). Show faith before you share faith. A caution here: don't let Jesus' encouragement make you fall for the nice-sounding-but-ultimately-false line of "preach the gospel always; when necessary, use words." No, the gospel *is* words, and if we don't say them, people won't know them. The gospel is a story, and if we don't tell it, people won't hear it. Matthew 5:16 is simply a wonderful reminder that we have the joy of showing the gospel as we share it.

Our privilege is in showing the gospel at the same time we share it.

Day Twelve
Matthew 5:21–26

....

We are now three days into the Sermon on the Mount, Jesus' master plan of discipleship that comprises Matthew 5–7. We began with the Beatitudes (5:1–12) and then Salt, Light, and Fulfillment (5:13–20).

Today, as they say in the South, Jesus stops preachin' and goes to meddlin'. He gets both personal and invasive as he deals in succession with anger, lust, marriage, and divorce. Today we'll focus on #1: anger.

Read 5:21–26 out loud. Go ahead; I'll wait. If you're worried you'll wake up someone in the house, whisper. If you're like me, reading it out loud makes you a bit frustrated with Jesus. Why? Do you see how quickly this escalates? After reminding us of the sort of ultimate "You shall not murder," Jesus then draws some of the most absurd parallels. "But I tell you" that if you are angry with your brother or sister. . . . Oh, you mean like road rage? You mean like a parking lot battle? You mean slow walkers? You mean everything necessary just to get to work on Monday morning?! That kind of anger will subject you to judgment? And then, "If you say 'Raca'. . . ." Why would I ever say *raca*? I don't even know what it means! And then I dug a little and discovered that *raca* was an ancient term calling someone empty-headed. Well, then I realize I've called people a lot worse than that—and so have you. What's the punishment? You call someone a "fool" and you're in danger of hell?! The escalation here implies a public shaming of both name and character. You rob another of their reputation. You take someone's good name and drag it through the mud, and AC/DC's song is your future because you're on the "Highway to Hell." All of a sudden any assurance you had of eternity in glory just vanished. What are you doing to us, Jesus?

It's funny to me (except the hell part). The passage escalates in the same way that our anger does. Have you ever noticed that? For a lot of you there is a fairly predictable pattern: annoyance to anger to rage to fury to explosion to nuclear meltdown to DEFCON 10. For some of you, the inciting incident is something with your kids. For others, it's your mate. Still for others, it's your parents, or coworkers, or a politician; and for a few of you, it's a preacher writing to you about anger.

Yet in the middle of that escalation, there is the language of verse 22: "angry with a brother or sister." Jesus subtly shifts to address anger that is less of an explosion and more of a lifestyle. What is lifestyle anger? It's when your anger is like a prize you won, your very reason for being, anger you nurse, cherish, and revisit. I suspect some of you know what that kind of anger is like. Perhaps you've never had the police come to your house to respond to an incident, but the anger about it is deep, enduring, and possessive. It's *your* anger, and it owns you as much as you own it. So many of us have lifestyle anger to one degree or another, and the thought that it will land us in damnation just seems worthy of a collective eye roll: "Jesus, I know what you're saying here, but I don't really believe it."

Remember the core conviction, Context Is Everything? You've no doubt learned to appreciate the subtlety of Jesus' language in Matthew's hands from the passage above. Now look at what happens in verses 23–24:

> "Therefore, if you are offering your gift at the altar and there remember that your brother or sister has something against you, leave your gift there in front of the altar. First go and be reconciled to them; then come and offer your gift."

As a preacher, I would say that if that offering is big enough, I don't care how many enemies you've got! Give it anyway! But do you see what has happened between verses 22 and 23? Do you see the twist? In the first collection of verses, it's about *your anger*. In the next, it turns to the ones *you anger*. It moves from you as *offended* to you as *offender*.

The twist continues in verses 25–26, in which a neighbor is taking you to court. In this brilliant way, the verse shifts from all the anger you *have* to all the anger you *cause*. Maybe you ought to go settle up with that person or those people so *they* don't go to hell! What a change in perspective if you're reading closely, paying attention, and loving the Scripture! You can't read one half of this passage without reading the other; it just doesn't work.

Here's a takeaway: Your anger fades when you face the ones you anger. You won't get so offended when you come face-to-face with all those times you have been an offender. You'll be less angry when you take a breath and realize just how many you have angered. The key to this section is moving from focus on your anger to the ones you anger.

What should we do with all of this today? Perhaps you have a former friend or an ex-spouse, and with a flash of insight you realize the anger you have caused him or her. You've been loving the anger you have but ignoring the anger you caused. Is it time for a text, a call, a note, or even a simple prayer of repentance?

I believe that when you allow Jesus to level the playing field by exposing your own self-righteousness, you'll be better able to hear what he says next regarding the content of your thoughts and the duration of your relationships.

**Your anger fades when you face
the ones you anger.**

Day Thirteen
Matthew 5:27-37

....

At this stage of the Sermon on the Mount, Jesus uses a distinct rhetorical device: "You have heard that it was said . . . but I tell you . . ."

You'll see those words (or approximations thereof) in relation to murder (v. 21), adultery (v. 27), divorce (v. 31), oaths (v. 33), revenge (v. 33), and loving neighbors/hating enemies (v. 43). By now you know that repetition is the Bible's neon light, shouting out to all of us, "Pay attention to this!"

So, what does this "you have heard . . . but I tell you" pattern mean? Why does he use it so often, and what does he communicate with it? Most of all, what is Matthew's purpose in recording it so faithfully? It's an interesting question, because up to now in this Gospel, Jesus has been completing everything that is Israel. Now, in addition to fulfilling Old Testament Scripture and Jewish life, Jesus seems to be both correcting and upgrading the tradition he inherits as a child of Israel. It's vital to know that with all these *upgrades* in 5:21–48, Jesus is not only commenting on the Hebrew Scriptures but also correcting much of the contemporary commentary on those Scriptures by ancient rabbis. In other words, some of the first-century interpretations of the Hebrew Bible had come to have the same authority as the Hebrew Bible, and one of the things Jesus does here is to say, "Not so fast, my friends. The rabbis may interpret Scripture, but they're fallible. I inspired them in the first place, and I am anointed." Let's take a look at a few of Jesus' key explanations.

Adultery (5:27-30)

This section is one of those that justifiably strikes fear into the heart and mind of every young man, and many young women as well. Why? Jesus moves from the act of adultery to the much more common fantasy about it: "I tell you that anyone who looks at a woman lustfully has already committed adultery with her in his heart" (v. 28). Some of you are old enough to remember that when Jimmy Carter was running for president as a self-identified born-again Christian in 1976, he confessed this sin in a famous interview. I remember how at age fourteen and not a Christian yet, his confession somehow made sense to me, and the ridicule he received for it seemed unfair. Of course, by today's standards in both parties, Carter's confession is tame indeed. Beyond presidential politics, what is Jesus saying here? This: where your mind dwells determines how your life goes. The glance, the observation, that natural impulse: not sinful. The obsession, the plan, the life you live in your head where you objectify those you find attractive: danger. The section ends with hyperbole. Jesus' original audience knew they were neither to remove their eyes nor amputate their hands. Jesus exaggerates the penalty to emphasize the point.

Divorce (5:31–32)

As you read these two verses, notice what's missing. Go ahead. I'll be patient. Right! No mention of how a woman may divorce her husband! That omission is the key to what's behind these words. In ancient Israel, as well as among the Romans who were occupying Israel by force, women were property to be embraced and discarded at will. The "certificate of divorce" in verse 31 could be accomplished literally overnight and for a cause as minor as a poorly cooked meal or a bad hair day (okay, I might have invented that second one). Through it all, Jesus declares that what the rabbis have diminished with their interpretations of Scripture he seeks to elevate by reminding them that marriage is God's idea, not theirs. He will have much more to say on the matter in Matthew 19, where he will resist the opportunity to redefine marriage and will reinforce it instead.

Oaths (5:33–37)

In ancient Israel, the different level of oaths involved in agreements between men (and yes, it was only men in that time) all suggested the degree to which they believed God was involved—or not—in the transaction. That's why men could swear by their "head" (v. 36). It was a way of saying, "This agreement is serious but not ultimate. I'm not swearing by God, so the stakes aren't very high, and my word might not be quite so dependable." Jesus calls them on their foolishness here and reminds them that all of life is under God's reign. No matter between people is too small for God. The integrity of a life of faith will influence conversations about and promises within every arena of life, from the legal to the moral to the spiritual. By letting our "Yes" or "No" actually mean what they say (v. 37), we avoid all the emotional energy we expend when we try to cover our lies.

*Where your mind dwells
determines how your life goes.*

Day Fourteen
Matthew 5:38-48

Today's reading brings to a close the section within the "Sermon on the Mount" that follows the "You have heard that it was said . . . but I tell you" pattern. This closing movement of this section focuses on two of the most famous "You have heard" sayings of them all: turn the other cheek (5:39) and love your enemies (v. 44). I will deal with each briefly before looking at that strange command at the end (v. 48) and then a principle of reading sections like this that I have found enormously helpful.

Eye for eye, tooth for tooth, turn the other cheek (5:38-42)

Perhaps you've heard the tale of the retired boxer who went into street preaching. One day while engaged in that ministry, he encountered a heckler who had the nerve to approach him and slug him on the cheek. Obediently, the boxer-turned-preacher offered the man his other cheek. The antagonist complied and slugged that one too. The boxer-turned-preacher then announced, "The Lord gave no further instructions," took off his coat, balled up his fist, and POW!

Street preaching aside, here's what you need to know when looking at these verses: "eye for eye, and tooth for tooth" (v. 38; Exod. 21:24) actually served to limit revenge in the ancient world. It made warfare between tribes and villages proportional. The tendency in ancient warfare was disproportional. If a neighboring people killed one of your soldiers, the first impulse in revenge was to slaughter the entire village. So the Hebrew command actually served to limit and to restrain. Yet Jesus enhances even that restraint and transforms a "thou shalt not" kind of command into a glimpse of a life of extravagant generosity.

"Love your enemies and pray for those who persecute you" (5:43-47).

Most of us have no desire to love our enemies. Some of us keep an "Enemies List." Others of us unfriend our enemies. A few of us block our enemies (that's really serious). Especially for those of us who have a list of enemies—either a mental list or one we document—here's what we fail to realize: the longer the list we keep, the more lists we're on. Gulp.

Notice what Jesus says in addition to "love your enemies": "pray for those who persecute you" (v. 44). Who is his audience? The disciples first, then the crowds. What will his disciples be subjected to after his departure? Relentless persecution. Except for John, none lived to old age; they all died at the hands of their persecutors. So Jesus was preparing them for the assaults they'd receive and offering some almost preposterous advice: "When those guys are killing you . . . pray for them." Again, where would we get such strength to live that way?

I find it helpful to remember what Paul says to the Roman church: "While we were God's enemies, we were reconciled to him through the death of his Son" (Rom. 5:10). With that verse in Romans, these words in Matthew open up to us. The only way to love your enemies is to realize that you're the loved enemy. You've been an enemy of the worst kind, an enemy of God. When you realize that about you—and how God moves to restore what you have broken— it opens up all kinds of relational possibilities.

The Final Command (5:48)

Jesus concludes a string of seemingly impossible commands with the most impossible of them all: "Be perfect, therefore, as your heavenly Father is perfect." Two things to note as we make sense of this: (1) it's a riff on Leviticus 11:45, where the Lord tells the Jews, "Be holy, because I am holy." *Holy* there means "different" or "set apart for a purpose." That was the role of the Jews. And as the fulfillment of all that is Israel, that's the role of Jesus' people as well. If you turn your other cheek and love your enemies, believe me: you'll be different! (2) I've also found it helpful to realize that Jesus speaks less about performance here than about position. In other words, you'll never have perfect performance for Jesus, but you do have perfect position in him. Hallelujah for that.

The Power for All This

The danger for any preacher or teacher of these words is to turn them into a series of *moralisms*: don't do this; do that. That's not only annoying and impossible; it's not Jesus' point. We make these passages about us, when in fact they are about Jesus.

Why do I say that? Well, read closely and note what is happening in this remarkable collection of sayings: Jesus *becomes* the stories he tells.

What do I mean by that? Well, look again at the examples in Matthew 5: they are conditional. "If your neighbor hits you," "if he take your clothes," "if he makes you walk a mile." If. If. If. Guess what? For Jesus, they became not hypothetical but actual. He's the one who is beaten and doesn't fight back. He's the one who is stripped naked. He is the one who is conscripted to carry his own cross. He's the one who gives. This little avalanche of nonsensical demands becomes so much more about him than us. What a storyteller! What a Savior! At every point, Jesus had the right—legal and divine—to assert his power and to insist on his respect. And at every step—trial, sentence, scourging, road to Golgotha, crucifixion—he didn't use the power available to him. He refused to assert his rights because he had to win our redemption. He was never more assertive than when he refused the power at his command and when he ignored the rights that were his.

Jesus becomes stories he tells and the sermon he preaches. Praise his name forever.

Day Fifteen
Matthew 6:1-18

Today's reading is a marvelous example of how Jesus in Matthew's hands uses both repetition and patterns to talk about much more than he is talking about. I know I have been *repetitive* in talking about Scripture's use of *repetition*, but the phenomenon keeps *repeating*! So as you read, prepare for more of the same, and know Matthew's purpose is not to bore you but alert you. The repetition is this:

Do not be like the hypocrites (6:2, 5, 16). Instead, practice much of your faith in private (vv. 1, 6, 18). Such private devotion leads to public reward (vv. 4, 6b, 18b).

The topics Jesus addresses—generosity (vv. 1–4), prayer (vv. 5–15), and fasting (vv. 16–18)—are really just cover for what he is actually talking about. Is your faith designed to bring honor to you or glory to God? Is it for display or done from devotion? These are serious matters and ones in which the Judaism of Jesus' time was failing. I suspect the Christianity of our time often fails as well.

What does Jesus seek to prevent in all his warnings about putting our religious practices on display? Being "like the hypocrites." The word *hypocrite* comes from a Greek term that means "actor." How can we ensure that we're not merely actors or posers when it comes to our faith? How does it instead flow from a place of authenticity?

I know from experience the wasted energy that comes from exhorting people, "Be authentic! Be genuine!" You can't command a sense of wonder and appreciation. Instead, you can merely evoke it. In light of that, I invite you to savor the unchanging truths of Jesus' life. In my own times of prayer, I have taken to writing down these signature moments in Jesus' life:

– **Incarnation**—infinity took on infancy in Bethlehem's manger.

– **Instruction**—the Word who became flesh then taught us in words we can't forget.

– **Crucifixion**—he who had no sin became sin for us.

– **Resurrection**—he is not here . . . he is risen!

– **Completion**—Jesus really is coming back to judge the quick and the dead.

These facets of Jesus' life give flavor to yours. When you ponder that, soak in it, and delight in it, no one has to tell you to be authentic. Your authenticity flows from his authority. This applies to how you give, how you pray, and even how you fast. Next we'll see how Jesus digs deeper into what we truly treasure in life.

***

**Savoring the truths of Jesus' life
adds flavor to yours.**

***

Day Sixteen
Matthew 6:19-24

Today's section is short in length but strong in impact. It's also an interesting case of how, once again, the Bible is not a book but a library. Today, we'll take a look at how Jesus' biographers arranged the material to suit their particular ends. Here in Matthew, the words we explore come from chapter 6 and occur in the middle of the Sermon on the Mount (Matthew 5–7). Luke places them later in his Gospel, most especially in 12:33–34, where they are part of the commentary following the parable of the rich fool (12:13–21).

Asking, "Well, who is right? When exactly did Jesus say these words about money and power?" is the wrong question. Ask instead, "What inspired Luke to place it in that context?" and "What inspired Matthew to put it in the Sermon on the Mount?" Those are the right questions. When you allow the Bible to be what it is, an often wild and woolly library with authors who are literary geniuses in their own right, then Bible study becomes both more interesting and more rewarding.

Today, we will look at three small paragraphs (6:19–21, 22–23, 24) in Matthew that cover much of the same territory. Their themes are Treasure, Eyes, and Masters.

Treasures (6:19–21)

Jesus begins this teaching moment with "Do not store up for yourselves treasures on earth, where moths and vermin destroy, and where thieves break in and steal" (v. 19). Jesus uses such vivid language: moths, vermin, and thieves. This is much more powerful and memorable than simply saying, "If you buy a bunch of stuff, you'll spend so much time worrying about your stuff that you'll miss out on what's important. It's all going to burn anyway." Whether you use the vivid imagery or the plain language, isn't the truth the same? The more you buy, the more time you spend protecting what you have bought! At the end of all days, it really will all burn up. The summary Jesus offers? "For where your treasure is, there your heart will be also" (v. 21).

Eyes (6:22–23)

Of these three paragraphs, this one is the least known but perhaps the most applicable: "If your eyes are unhealthy, your whole body will be full of darkness" (v. 23). This is really an expansion of Jesus' conversation on adultery and lust in Matthew 5:27–30. If you don't monitor your eyes, you will naturally fall into this pattern: *See, want, get.* Untrained eyes desire to acquire all they see, from possessions to acclaim to people we find sexually attractive. This is Samson's great sin and why Samson is no hero despite what your children's Bible may have told you. Advertisers make their hay by appealing to our eyes; pornographers, tragically, do the same. It's so much better and healthier to train your brain to avert your eyes and curb your appetites.

Masters (6:24)

Talk about a summary statement on divided loyalties! "No one can serve two masters. Either you will hate the one and love the other, or you will be devoted to the one and despise the other" (v. 24). Jesus is not asking you to choose between polar opposites. It's not "good versus bad." It's "good versus much better" or "urgent versus ultimate."

Like most preachers, I have found (and I teach) that the weekly rhythm of generosity is the best method of controlling our tendency to hoard. It's God's brilliant strategy to help us make and keep priorities. But there's something more than that, and it's related to the *savoring* truths I referenced in yesterday's reading. When you ponder and celebrate the degree to which you have been chased, bought, and kept, then how can you do anything but give well to the One who gave all?

**I'd rather become his possession
than count up mine.**

Day Seventeen
Matthew 6:25–34

....

I'm excited today, because I get to teach most of you a new word. The word is: *inclusio.*

What does *inclusio* mean? It's a fancy word for "bookends." It is a literary structure biblical authors often use to reinforce what they're talking about. When a section of Scripture begins and ends with the same phrase or idea, then you know to read everything in the middle in light of either end. One of the more famous is Psalm 8, which begins and concludes with "LORD, our Lord, how majestic is your name in all the earth!" (vv. 1, 9). Whatever else that psalm is about, it's about the majesty of the Lord's name: *Inclusio.*

Matthew 6:25–34 is a classic example of *inclusio*. Here it is:

6:25: "Therefore I tell you, do not worry about your life . . ."

6:34: "Therefore do not worry about tomorrow . . ."

Well, guess what this section of the Sermon on the Mount is about? Worry, stress, anxiety. That sounds a lot like life in the 2020s.

With that introduction and conclusion, Jesus goes on to draw a series of analogies, all designed to increase his followers' faith and decrease their anxiety. The first is the birds of the air, what they eat, and how they don't hoard. The summary? "Are you not much more valuable than they"? (v. 26).

The second analogy is like the first: instead of birds of the air, it's the flowers of the field (v. 28) and how they are clothed in splendor (v. 29). Again, if the flowers—which by definition are temporary—receive clothing, will not we who are eternal receive the same?

Now, if you're like me, you're not especially happy about this series of commands or the analogies that support them. Worry is second nature. How can Jesus tell us not to do something that feels both natural and effortless?

In recent years, one quotation has really helped me get a handle on my own worry and harness that same energy into something more productive.

It's the saying I have heard making the rounds recently: "Worry is praying to yourself." To that I'd add: "and you're a terrible god." Can I hear an amen?

To that helpful observation, I'd add one more, something that is embedded within the *inclusio* of Matthew 6:25–34. It's the gorgeous line of verse 33: "But seek first his kingdom and his righteousness, and all these things will be given to you as well."

Matthew 6:33 offers a profound truth. The harder you strive for happiness, the more elusive it becomes. When you strive for godliness—say, for example, by coming to life through Bible study on an everyday basis—happiness as well as food and clothing and peace get thrown in.

....

Seek happiness more than godliness and you'll get neither. Seek godliness more than happiness and you'll get both.

....

Day Eighteen
Matthew 7:1-6

....

Are you ready for one of the most widely known and yet most misused sections of the Bible? Well, here it is! These words of Jesus have become ammunition against the church by people whose knowledge of Scripture is limited to this section. What's the refrain? "Don't judge me! Who are you to judge?" In response, people inside the church often pick up the same refrain whenever the subject of church accountability comes up.

What's really going on here? And how does the subject relate to the early church? It's one of those topics where Paul helps us to interpret Jesus.

First, there's this: "Do not judge, or you too will be judged. For in the same way you judge others, you will be judged, and with the measure you use, it will be measured to you" (vv. 1–2). So is Jesus speaking of divine judgment, as in what you dole out to others you can expect God to dole out to you? Or is it more relational in nature: when you are free with your assessment of other people, don't be surprised at a boomerang effect when people are free in their assessments of you? The setting and the tone appear to favor the latter understanding; this command has more horizontal application (your relations with others) than vertical (your connection with God), more of a natural consequence than divine retribution.

I say that because of what follows. "Why do you look at the speck of sawdust in your brother's eye and pay no attention to the plank in your own eye?" (v. 3). Digging further into what Jesus says here, we marvel at his challenge to grow in our self-awareness. Isn't it true that we are most critical of others in the very same area where we are weak and wounded ourselves? Isn't it true in matters small and large that those who yell the loudest have the most to hide?

All in all, the greatest obstacle to self-improvement is a focus on the flaws of others. It's the specks and the planks that show us. The summary statement of verse 5 is withering in its commentary: "You hypocrite, first take the plank out of your own eye, and then you will see clearly to remove the speck from your brother's eye." Indeed.

I mentioned Paul earlier. How does he fit into all this? Paul's ministry connects to Jesus' words in a way that's both surprising and unsettling. As he writes his first letter to the Corinthian church, he has to correct that congregation's spiritual preening by reminding them of the blatant sin they're allowing in their own midst: "It is actually reported that there is sexual immorality among you, and of a kind that even pagans do not tolerate: A man is sleeping with his father's wife" (1 Cor. 5:1). Paul is referring to the man's stepmother, not his biological one, but it elicits a collective *bleh* nonetheless. Paul moves on from there to recommend some severe discipline—"Expel the wicked person from among you" (v. 13), but along the way he offers this thought:

> What business is it of mine to judge those outside the church? Are you not to judge those inside? God will judge those outside. (vv. 12–13)

In other words, the church shouldn't spend time judging the culture; it should instead have sure and consistent discipline within its own ranks. It is ironic that for the most part we in church-land do the reverse in the modern era. We spend plenty of time calling out the sin that surrounds us while rationalizing away the sin within. Surely, when you take Matthew 7 and add some 1 Corinthians 5 to the mix, we find a wake-up call to the church as a whole to grow in its own self-awareness.

Do you spend time and energy judging those you don't know as a way of avoiding intimacy with those you do?

Day Nineteen
Matthew 7:7-14

Today we move off some perplexing words about judging and into some very encouraging words about praying. The words Jesus uses and the concepts he teaches have the ability to revolutionize the ways we pray. Let me show you what I mean.

He starts with "Ask and it will be given to you; seek and you will find; knock and the door will be opened to you" (v. 7). Ask. Seek. Knock. In other words, with great persistence, harass the Lord in prayer! Why? Because what's important is not the one knocking but the one on the other side of the door. Jesus is layering his teaching on prayer by telling his disciples about the character of the Father. And then Jesus goes on in verses 9–10: "Which of you, if your son asks for bread, will give him a stone? Or if he asks for a fish, will give him a snake?" In Luke 11, Jesus adds, "Or if he asks for an egg, will give him a scorpion?" (v. 12).

Think about what Jesus is saying: "Daddy, can I have a fish?" And the answer: "No, but how about rattler for dinner?" Or even: "Granddad, can I have an egg?" "No, sonny, but I've been saving this scorpion just for you!"

Who would answer that? No one who is not already in prison! Then there's the kicker from that strangest of analogies in 7:1: "If you, then, though you are evil, know how to give good gifts to your children, how much more will your Father in heaven give good gifts to those who ask him!" You know enough not to do that; then *how much more* does God treat you especially well!

We often want to know the system of prayer, but Jesus instead tells us about the source of our blessings. We want to know the process for prayer, and Jesus tells us about the power of God to bless us. Here are Jesus' claims: "Let me tell you about the Father: he is the one who will act consistently with his character, who won't humiliate you when you harass him; he's the one who is open before you even knock. He's not a grouch who gives his gifts reluctantly. He is a gem who gives them eagerly. And best of all, even if your daddy— whether a bad dad, okay dad, really good dad, the best dad—knows how to give you good stuff, lay that beside God's ability and desire, and there is no comparison!" Giving is God's love language! Answering prayer isn't God's duty. It's God's delight.

My father, Harvey Davis, was fifty years old when I was born (I am also the eighth of eight children). In thinking about him (he died in 2006 at the age of ninety-five), I recall the phenomenon of love languages, how the groundbreaking book by Gary Chapman (*The Five Love Languages*) revealed that some people express love through touch, while others use words, still others via service, and then some by spending quality time or giving special gifts. When it came to my father, we didn't go to him if we wanted to cuddle. That wasn't his style. By the same token, he wasn't one to tell us he loved us until we grew up and started telling him first. Did he serve us? Occasionally. Did he speak the language of quality time? No, because that would interfere with the Dallas Cowboys game he wanted to watch. But gifts? Oh, when I was eleven and came downstairs on my birthday, he reached behind his chair and said, "Here!" while he tossed me a red, white, and blue ABA basketball. Perfect! When I was twelve, it was Paul Simon's album with "Kodachrome" on it. More perfect. When I was thirteen, it was a peanut butter and jelly sandwich waiting for me in the backseat of his car when he'd pick me up from school to take me to practice tennis. Still more perfect. Gifts, gifts, gifts. He wasn't good at *saying* love, but he was great at *giving* it. Guess what? Even that, even the best my dad did, does not hold a candle to our Father in heaven. It's wired into God's DNA. Answering your prayer isn't God's duty. It's God's delight.

Here's what I want you to do when you close your Bible today. Smile when you pray. Literally. As you write your prayers or pray them silently or even recite the Lord's Prayer, do it with a smile. You know how contagious smiles are, don't you? As you smile when you pray, you're reflecting the smile on the face of your Father in heaven. Ask for what's big and bold and eternal: for someone you know is lost to be saved, for revival to break out in your community, for you to be filled with the Holy Spirit of God for the duties you face today. Pray in the spirit of Matthew 7:13–14 that more people will choose the "small . . . gate and narrow . . . road that leads to life." Do it with a smile because that's how God is already answering you.

**Answering your prayer isn't God's duty.
It's God's delight.**

Day Twenty
Matthew 7:15-23

Jesus uses this second-to-last section of the Sermon on the Mount not to comfort but to challenge and to warn. Look how he begins in Matthew 7:15: "Watch out for false prophets. They come to you in sheep's clothing, but inwardly they are ferocious wolves." Many of us in the twenty-first century run into an immediate interpretive problem with these words: we think biblical prophets are future predictors. By and large, they're not; they are truth tellers. Old Testament figures such as Isaiah and Jeremiah (major prophets) and Joel and Hosea (minor prophets) have some future orientation to them, but their primary role is telling Israel what it needs to know and do whether the nation likes it or not. The office of prophet was held in high esteem until said prophet ran afoul of the king, in which case trouble would come. Just ask Jeremiah. Or Ezekiel.

In the years of the early church, prophets also appeared in Jesus' name. We know from literature written around AD 100 that church leaders had to warn church members to be wary of wandering prophets. If a prophet's motive was greed and his method full of demands, the church's leaders would warn people to stay away. If a prophet's motive was truth and his method was proclamation, the church's leaders would advise people to lean in.

What does Jesus say? "By their fruit you will recognize them" (v. 16). Whether in traveling ministries or parish ministries, fruit reveals source. As I prayed on these words earlier and recognized the many ways that I want people to connect to the church I serve, I landed here:

> "Lord, make sure that I want the kind of fruit where people have a greater allegiance to you than loyalty to me."

This kind of prayer would appear to be self-evident, but I don't think I'm the only spiritual leader who struggles along these lines. I'm glad I read these words while preparing this study.

The second section of today's reading (vv. 21–23) is even more threatening. If verses 15–20 were about false prophets, verses 21–23 are about false disciples. "Not everyone who says to me, 'Lord, Lord,'" Jesus says, "will enter the kingdom of heaven, but only the one who does the will of my Father who is in heaven" (v. 21).

Is Jesus saying we earn our salvation by what we do as opposed to receiving it by what we say? If so, we have a real biblical dilemma, as Romans, Galatians, Ephesians, and others give us the clarion call of salvation by faith and not by works. So how do we make a cohesive whole out of the disparate sections of the New Testament library? In this case, it's vital to remember exactly what problem the authors were addressing. In those letters, Paul is dealing with those who sought to reinstate Jewish customs and religious rituals as the basis for faith in Jesus. He therefore had to be emphatic in saying that forgiveness comes from the blood of Jesus through faith. In Matthew 7, Jesus addresses those who follow him for the sake of spectacle, and those who want to use him as leverage for the next miracle. That's why verses 22–23 refer to the objections of the damned as revolving around "but we did stuff in your name!" What's missing in that kind of discipleship? Abiding. Remaining. Deep dependence on Christ, not as a commodity we leverage for personal gain, but as a Savior who rescues us from personal ruin.

The thread running throughout this section of Scripture connects false prophets with false disciples: Are we in it to grow our own platforms or increase his? To support our agenda or highlight his? For us to use Jesus or allow him to use us? With those hard questions, I can't wait to see just how he winds up this sermon.

Today is a great day to increase Jesus' platform rather than expand yours.

Day Twenty-One
Matthew 7:24-29

A s the Sermon on the Mount winds down, how will Jesus dismount? Will he stick his landing, à la Mary Lou Retton, Kerri Strug, or Simone Biles (choose your own Olympic heroine)? Absolutely!

I love the details of Jesus' closing illustration in Matthew 7:24: "Therefore everyone who hears these words of mine and puts them into practice is like a wise man who built his house on the rock." Notice he says *hears* and not *reads*. Why? Well, first, because it's near the end of a spoken sermon! Second, and I remind you of this again and again, the books of the biblical library were written to be heard out loud and not read silently, as most people in that era could not read. When you realize those are the assumptions behind almost all biblical authors, you'll be stunned at how often they write *hear* when you'd think *read*.

Now we return to the sermon closer at hand. When Jesus says "everyone who hears these words of mine," to what words does he refer? The words he's just spoken in the sermon! The beatitudes that begin it, the "turn the other cheek" and "love your enemies" in the next phase, the prayer, fasting, and generosity in the middle, and then the admonitions not to judge others but to discern the prophets in chapter 7. All of it. He means all of it.

Those who hear and do are like a wise man who builds his house upon a rock. What happens to that house? The rains, storms, and winds assault it mercilessly. The result? "[Y]et it did not fall, because it had its foundation on the rock" (v. 25). Stability, endurance, and perseverance are the results of building a life on Jesus.

Jesus then sets up an almost perfect contrast: "But everyone who hears these words of mine and does not put them into practice is like a foolish man who built his house on sand" (v. 26) What do we know about sand in ancient Israel? It was everywhere, as that land was and is surrounded by desert. Sand is deceptive because it looks stable and solid during the dry season but changes dramatically when it rains. Finally, it's easier to build a house on sand than rock, because the resistance is much less when you dig a foundation through porous sand rather than solid rock. So, Jesus is saying, "People who like the sound of my words but don't bother to build their lives upon them are vulnerable to the foundation the world offers: deceptive, quick, and easy." The two men in the story have a great contrast in the source of their foundations.

What do they have in common? The first part of verse 27 tells us: "The rain came down, the streams rose, and the winds blew and beat against that house." That's the exact same language as in verse 25. The connecting thread for the lazy and disciplined alike are that storms come. Storms in your life and mine are inevitable. The difference comes in the foundation on which that life is built. What happens to Sand Guy, who chose a foundation that was easier and quicker? "And it fell with a great crash" (v. 27). Jesus literally ends his sermon with a *boom*. He nails the landing.

The implication? Jesus wants to be foundation and not decoration.

Having Jesus as a decoration in your life is relatively easy; you put some nice sayings on the wall, you have a large family Bible on the coffee table (open, but never read), and you go to him when you're in a crisis. When he is foundation, that Bible is actually read and its commandments followed. You continually ask, "What does the Lord want to do in me and through me in this situation?" You allow yourself to savor the depth of his relentless love for you, and you realize that the consistent obedience to inconvenient truths like tithing, forgiveness, and quiet time will help you prevent crises rather than manage them. You have stability.

The crowds in verses 28–29 are "amazed" at the depth and authority of Jesus' teachings. Let's join with the ancients in our wonder.

*It's easy to make Jesus a decoration in your home.
It's right to make him the foundation of it.
Choose what's right over what's easy.*

Day Twenty-Two
Matthew 8:1-17

J esus has just finished the "Sermon on the Mount" (Matt. 5–7). How will he follow that up? Sunday lunch at Luby's Cafeteria? Sunday dinner at his grandmother's house? An afternoon in front of the TV? Well, not exactly.

Instead, Matthew describes a flurry of activity in which Jesus' healing power underscores the authority of the words he has just spoken. Notice what happens first: "When Jesus came down from the mountainside, large crowds followed him" (8:1). That's a refreshing observation, as the source of the crowd's interest is not Jesus' miracles (those are coming) but his message. Perhaps they heard the closing words of the Sermon on the Mount (7:24–27) and decided to build their lives on rock and not on sand.

While miracles didn't draw this crowd, they certainly will have a role in keeping it. The first involves a man with leprosy who pleads with Jesus: "Lord, if you are willing, you can make me clean" (8:2). Jesus declares his willingness to heal as well as his authority over leprosy, and the man's skin is "immediately" cleansed (8:3). Jesus' closing instruction in Matthew 8:4 involves an elaborate process of offering and purification described in Leviticus 14. Priests in those days did triple duty as butchers, dermatologists, and representatives of the Lord! With his fidelity to ancient practices, Jesus again reminds us that he has come not to contradict what had been given to the Jews but to complete it.

The next healing story, in verses 5–13, reveals that although Jesus is the fulfillment of all that is Israel, his mission will impact Gentiles as well. We read this in verse 5: "When Jesus had entered Capernaum, a centurion came to him, asking for help. 'Lord,' he said, 'my servant lies at home paralyzed, suffering terribly.'" What is a *centurion*? A Roman soldier, meaning a Gentile, a worshiper of pagan gods, and a member of the occupying force terrorizing Israel. Jesus ministers to the enemy. Once again, he becomes the stories he tells and the truths he utters.

Jesus will later (v. 10) commend this man's faith, and on the surface, it will be because he has ultimate trust in Jesus' ability to heal. Yet I think the man's great act of faith is in his first word to Jesus: "Lord." If you're a Roman soldier, "Caesar is Lord," and there is no other! If the wrong person had heard him affirm Jesus as Lord, his superiors in the Roman army would have executed him as a traitor. The stakes were that high for everyone living under Roman domination, but especially so for soldiers in the regime.

The back-and-forth between this soldier and our Savior in verses 8–12 continues the dual theme of Jesus' authority and the broadening scope of his mission. Notice the language of verses 11–12. Luke uses those same words in his Gospel (Luke 13:29). In both places, they're a sobering reminder that if the children of Israel reject their messiah, the Lord will bring in Gentiles from around the globe to take their seats at the kingdom feast. The end result of this encounter? "And his servant was healed at that moment" (v. 13), a healing that occurs *offstage* so that Jesus can remain *center stage*.

The final scene in this healing triplicate takes place in Simon Peter's Capernaum home, where his mother-in-law is "lying in bed with a fever" (v. 14). I want to ask, "Peter, why are your in-laws living with you?" but that's only because I am a modern American and not an ancient Jew. Such arrangements were typical in that day.

Mark's Gospel has a parallel scene in 1:29–34. The fact that it is in Mark 1 while this is in Matthew 8 is yet another example of how those two Gospel authors tell the same story in basically the same order, but Matthew supplies much more detail and displays much less urgency. Yet, whether it's Mark's frenetic pacing or Matthew's more measured approach, we see the same truths revealed:

No problem is too small for Jesus' attention (he heals Peter's mother-in-law).

No problem is too big for Jesus' ability (he heals the crowd, at night!).

No problem is too stubborn for Jesus' authority (he casts out evil spirits).

....

No problem is too small for Jesus' attention, no problem is too big for his ability, and no problem is too stubborn for his authority.

....

Day Twenty-Three

Matthew 8:18–22

In yesterday's reading, Jesus first heals a centurion's servant and then delivers many in the entire village of Capernaum. Tomorrow, we'll see him calming a storm and freeing two men from demon possession. This section is full of miracles. We've gone from Jesus the *sage* in the Sermon on the Mount to Jesus the *sensation* in the towns and villages on the plain.

With all that, these two encounters in Matthew 8:18–22 seem out of place. Two men make bold promises about following Jesus, and in both cases it looks as if Jesus pours cold water on their boldness. What's all that about, and why does Matthew place these vignettes in this miracle section? I'll deal with the second question first.

The key to the question, "Why these encounters in the middle of the miracles?" lies in verse 19: "Then a teacher of the law came to him and said, 'Teacher, I will follow you wherever you go.'" Other translations render "teacher of the law" as "scribe," as in the "scribes and Pharisees," Jesus' opponents. This is indeed miraculous! One of Jesus' sworn enemies has decided to follow him. A teacher of the law calls Jesus "Teacher." What looks out of place becomes, when you think about it, among the greatest miracles of them all.

So why does Jesus not encourage him? I would have answered, "Well, come on then! We have vibrant worship services and ministries for the whole family!" But Jesus' answer is this: "Foxes have dens and birds have nests, but the Son of Man has no place to lay his head" (v. 20). What's going on?

Jesus wants the man to count the cost. He wants this teacher of the law to know there's a whole lot of new material he'll need to master. He'll be entering the upside-down, save-your-life-by-losing-it, greatness-through-serving realm of the kingdom of God. No one ever accused Jesus of overpromising and under-delivering.

At first glance, the second encounter is more troubling: "Another disciple said to [Jesus], 'Lord, first let me go and bury my father.' But Jesus told him, 'Follow me, and let the dead bury their own dead'" (vv. 21–22).

Pastors, do not under any circumstances utter this line when asked to do a funeral. Never.

Two things to note. First, this man is already a "disciple" who calls Jesus "Lord." Could he be one of the Twelve? Or one of his outer ring of followers? We don't know because Matthew doesn't say. Nevertheless, this man is already *in*.

Second, we have no indication the man's father had died. In ancient times, the line about burying a parent could also mean: "I need to fulfill all my obligation to my father's house, and only when he dies am I free to choose my own way of life." This disciple may well have been saying, "I'm putting your cause on pause, Jesus. I've got responsibilities at home, and when my dad eventually dies, then I'll be back at your service." This disciple wants to follow Jesus partially, on his terms, not on Jesus' conditions. He might as well say, "I'd like to be a part-time disciple!" But for Jesus, partial following is complete rejection.

So, what is this all about? Jesus never promises easy or swift or glib. He just offers real. Have you counted the cost of following Jesus?

The world offers glib. Jesus counteroffers with real. Whose offer will you accept?

Day Twenty-Four
Matthew 8:23-34

....

After an interlude in which the greatest miracle was a scribe who wanted to follow Jesus, Matthew now returns with two more stories demonstrating Jesus' power over both the natural and the supernatural. The parallels are in Mark 4:35–5:18, a rare case in which he is more expansive than Matthew.

Look how Matthew begins his version: "Then he got into the boat and his disciples followed him. Suddenly a furious storm came up on the lake, so that the waves swept over the boat. But Jesus was sleeping" (8:23–24). These types of storms are typical in the Sea of Galilee, as it is tucked in a *bowl* surrounded by hillsides. In fact, the disciples—professional fishermen, after all—probably knew the weather patterns well enough to warn Jesus not to get into the boat at this time of day.

Yet Jesus sleeps through the storm. The disciples wake him in verse 25 with "Lord, save us! We're going to drown!" (Mark's version has them ask, "Don't you care if we drown?" 4:38). Jesus responds by rebuking the men and then the storm. The storm obeys more comprehensively than the men: "and it was completely calm" (v. 26). The weather is calm but "the men were amazed" (v. 27). The Greek word Matthew uses to emphasize the disciples' fear translates as "agitated," a brilliant way of suggesting that they were more scared of the calm than of the storm! In the calm, they would have to deal with Jesus alone in the boat. In the storm, their problems function as a distraction from their relationship with Jesus.

Did you catch that? Many of us prefer the storm to the calm. When it's calm, we are alone with Jesus. When life brings a storm, or when we chase one down and make it our own, we can distract ourselves from Jesus and dwell on our own problems.

In any event, the men ask the question of questions: "What kind of man is this" (v. 27)? At this stage, it is vital to remember that we know something the disciples do not: Jesus is the Messiah, the Son of the living God. We've been told that from the beginning, but the disciples have only a growing awareness of it. What kind of man is this carpenter turned rabbi? Answer #1: the kind of man who has power over nature. He can calm a storm, which may even imply that he sent it in the first place.

Answer #2 to the same question is the subject of the next scene. On the other side of the lake, Jesus and his entourage encounter "two demon-possessed men coming from the tombs . . . [who] were so violent that no one could pass that way" (v. 28). Look at their first words: "What do you want with us, Son of God?" (v. 29). See that? They know Jesus' identity before the disciples do! The disciples ask, "What kind of man is this?" Voilà! In the next scene, Matthew answers that question through the voice of the demonic.

The demons within the men know who and what they are up against and beg Jesus to drive them out. Is this the desire of the men to be relieved from such possession? Is it simply a case of Satan's legions meeting their match? We're not sure. All we know is that Jesus responds with one word: "Go!" (v. 32). The demons obey, rushing into a herd of pigs (unclean animals in Hebrew thinking and teaching) and from there into destruction. The men themselves are saved and healed.

What kind of man is this? Answer #2: one who has authority over the supernatural. In both scenes, we see that no realm is beyond Jesus' authority: the natural world of weather and storms and the supernatural one of demons and spirits.

The response of the villagers is, in its own way, like the response of the men in the boat: "And when they saw him, they pleaded with him to leave their region" (v. 34). You know what that tells us? The villagers liked it when the men were demon possessed. They were familiar with it. It was comfortable. It may have been dysfunctional, but they were used to it. Now? The men have been delivered, but the villagers are disturbed! The healing of the men upsets their equilibrium. Their solution is to get rid of the problem, the agitator: Jesus the Messiah.

Have we become so used to storms and panic that we prefer them over peace and calm? Whether in our own lives or the lives of others, have we accepted what is ultimately unacceptable? Do we nurse our issues and relish our problems because they give us a sense of identity? If Jesus were to heal and deliver us completely, how would we feel?

....
Are you a storm chaser? If you waver in your answer, ask someone you love, "Do I chase storms?"
....

Day Twenty-Five
Matthew 9:1-8

M atthew 9 ushers in a section of this book in which Jesus will face ever-growing opposition. Jesus' words, actions, and authority threaten both religious and political leaders in occupied Israel, which will ultimately nail him to the cross.

Before he gets there, however, he has much ministry to embrace. Here's how this section begins: "Jesus stepped into a boat, crossed over and came to his own town" (9:1). You might think that "his own town" is Nazareth. Not so. In fact, it's Capernaum, as Matthew 4:13 has already told us.

For the second story in a row, Matthew actually provides less detail than Mark, an unusual fact given that his Gospel is roughly twice the length. Mark tells us that this encounter takes place in a house and that the man whom Jesus heals has been lowered by his friends through the roof. No such drama, or truss damage, in Matthew:

> Some men brought to him a paralyzed man, lying on a mat. When Jesus saw their faith, he said to the man, "Take heart, son; your sins are forgiven." (v. 2)

I find myself wondering about "their" faith. Whose faith is Matthew describing? The friends'? The man himself? All of them? We don't know for sure, though the *faith* focus has consistently dwelt on the friends. They are the ones who have identified Jesus as the source of healing and have carried their friend some distance to see him. If you're a Christian today, it's because someone *brought* you to him; whether you suffered paralysis or not, you were pretty helpless before Jesus' saving intervention in your life.

The audacity of Jesus' words regarding forgiveness of sins generates some predictable opposition: "At this, some of the teachers of the law said to themselves, 'This fellow is blaspheming!'" (v. 3). If you look back at 8:19, one of those same "teachers of the law" promised to follow Jesus wherever he went! Ah, the fickleness of religious leaders!

Matthew 9:4 is so subtle: "Knowing their thoughts . . ." Could there be a more emphatic declaration of Jesus' divinity? In some ways, that's even more dramatically *divine* than either the ability to forgive sins or to heal paralysis, both of which will be revealed next. Jesus knows thoughts. Then and now. After this moment of knowing, Jesus asks the question at the center of the entire encounter: "Which is easier: to say, 'Your sins are forgiven,' or to say, 'Get up and walk'?" (v. 5).

Well, which is easier? The answer: neither. But they are inherently related, as verse 6 says: "But I want you to know that the Son of Man has authority on earth to forgive sins." This healing is secondary to the authority it conveys. The same Jesus who has authority over the weather (8:23–27) and the demonic (8:28–34) now has authority over the deepest problem in the human race, sin itself (9:1–8). This healing serves to verify the scandalous words Jesus has uttered.

I love the understated tone of the healing itself: "So he said to the paralyzed man, 'Get up, take your mat and go home.' Then the man got up and went home" (vv. 7–8). No fluff, no extra drama, "just the facts, ma'am." Those who witness it praise God, "who had given such authority to man" (v. 9). There's that word again. *Authority* has been tested, questioned, proven, displayed, and now praised.

How far are you willing to go to bring someone to Jesus?

Day Twenty-Six
Matthew 9:9-13

This short passage is loaded with meaning and impact. It is always interesting to consider the role of autobiography in each of the Gospel accounts. To what degree do the authors insert themselves into the story, and how do they do so? With John, for example, most readers through the centuries have regarded the mysterious "disciple whom Jesus loved" as John himself. Luke waits until his own volume 2, the book of Acts, before placing himself in the narrative. Mark is possibly the naked guy in 14:51–52 of the Gospel that bears his name, but that is more conjecture than certainty.

Matthew does it with a third-person narrative in which he doesn't hide the identity of *Matthew* but never uses either the first-person pronoun (I/me/mine) or a subtle turn of phrase to do so. His narrator is omniscient, and the author becomes a character in the story. What kind of character? The kind no self-respecting person would tolerate. Look at Matthew 9:9: "As Jesus went on from there, he saw a man named Matthew sitting at the tax collector's booth. 'Follow me,' he told him, and Matthew got up and followed him."

Why would I say no self-respecting person would be seen in Matthew's presence? Because he was a Jew who had sold his soul to the occupying Roman Empire by collecting taxes from his own people and for his sworn enemy. He was a traitor—worse, a traitor who had likely grown rich at the expense of his own countrymen and for the benefit of his oppressors. Given that Jesus encounters Matthew "as [he] went on from there," it seems likely that Matthew collected a "travel tax"—like those newfangled express lanes on superhighways across our land, only it was neither computerized nor standardized. Matthew had negotiated an arrangement with the Romans that he would collect a specified amount. Whatever he could extort on top of that was his. This is a bad man.

Yet Jesus' first words are "Follow me." Not "Get it together, dude." Not "Come to the altar." Not "Start tithing and then we'll talk." Not even "Hey Matthew, I'd love to have you on my team, but what would others think?" Just the simple: "Follow me."

Matthew "got up and followed him." Think of all it doesn't say! What were Matthew's emotions? What did his parents say? What happened to the funds he'd collected? Was Judas the one person in the inner circle who was pleased, since he was in charge of the money? We don't know because Matthew doesn't say.

What we do know is that Jesus not only calls him but also enters his house to eat with him (v. 10). In the spirit of the day, Matthew brings his sketchy, tax-collector friends with him! The company Jesus keeps here alarms the Pharisees, and in one of the most passive-aggressive moves in history, they ask Jesus' disciples about it: "Why does your teacher eat with tax collectors and sinners?" (v. 11).

The disciples receive the question, but Jesus provides the answer. He responds to passive aggression with clarity and honesty: "It is not the healthy who need a doctor, but the sick. But go and learn what this means: 'I desire mercy, not sacrifice.' For I have not come to call the righteous, but sinners" (vv. 12–13). The "mercy, not sacrifice" there comes from Hosea 6:6 and is, yet again, a way for Jesus to confirm that he fulfills all that is Israel, not as a ritual to be practiced but as a life to be lived. When he tells the Pharisees that his calling is for the sinners and not for the righteous, they must have breathed a sigh of relief: "Whew! He's not talking about us, then, because everybody knows we're righteous." That particular sigh of relief will prove to be spectacularly wrong.

This passage is, instead, spectacularly good news for all of us with a past, which means all of us. You've never gone too far or done too much or become too despised for Jesus to say to you, "Follow me." All he wants is for you to have the self-awareness to place yourself among "the sinners" apart from him and then among "the sanctified" in him.

That's what Matthew did. He got up and left behind his past, his fortune, and his skeletons. In fact, it appears that the only thing he took with him was his pen, the one he used to write this incomparable tale.

You've never gone too far or done too much or become too despised for Jesus to say to you, "Follow me."

Day Twenty-Seven
Matthew 9:14-17

We're reading a short section of Scripture today, but one yet again loaded with meaning and application. By now we know enough about Jesus' life and Matthew's portrayal of it that anytime Jesus asserts or proves his authority, he can expect opposition.

This time it comes from an unlikely source: "Then John's disciples came and asked him, 'How is it that we and the Pharisees fast often, but your disciples do not fast?" (9:14). What a subtle detail! The question comes not from scribes or Pharisees, but from the followers of Jesus' first cousin! The question contains more than a hint of spiritual pride: Jesus, why aren't your followers as faithful as we are?

Jesus' answer involves a rhetorical question regarding Jewish wedding customs: "How can the guests of the bridegroom mourn while he is with them? The time will come when the bridegroom will be taken from them; then they will fast" (v. 15). In ancient Israel (and even in modern India, among other places), wedding ceremonies were spread out over several days. It was a time of celebration for even the humblest of families, and rejoicing was the norm. Jesus compares himself to the bridegroom and his own disciples to the friends at the weeklong party. "Time for sorrow and lament is coming," Jesus is saying, "but it's not now." The Christian faith, then, doesn't deny sorrow but perseveres through it.

Jesus' second analogy expands on the first; in verses 16–17, he compares his presence with both patched cloth and wineskins. Of the two metaphors, the *wineskins* has received much more attention in the history of the church. Ancient peoples stored their wine in leather skins as opposed to glass bottles. If you stored new wine in an older, brittle skin, the fermentation process still occurring in that new wine would make the brittle skin burst, the wine would spill, and the drink would be wasted. New wine needed to be stored in a new skin that still had elasticity.

Jesus' incarnation and his message are the "new wine" in this analogy. Such a radically new message could not be contained in many of the brittle religious practices Israel had layered over the Jewish faith. In many ways, Jesus' words here prepare his followers for their ultimate expulsion from the synagogue (which will happen in the book of Acts) and the embrace of this new gathering called *the church*.

How do these words intersect with us today? Well, first, here is what Jesus (and the historic church) is not saying; he is not saying that our message must continually change. There is no *new gospel*. We don't invent a new faith every generation; we inherit it from those who have preceded us.

Yet no single container can ever contain that priceless message. The skins in which we store the wine of the faith must never become brittle. All this explains dozens of innovations in the world of the church, from the sixteenth-century innovation of the printing press, leading to Bibles in your home, to online pandemic church in the twenty-first century. Through it all, the message does not change—God help us if it does—but the methods do. We're in the middle of just such a "new wineskin" now; not only do you have your own copy of the Bible in your home (incomprehensible until the 1500s), but you're likely part of many communities who interact primarily through cyberspace rather than face-to-face. Through it all, God is good.

An old saying goes this way: "Traditionalism is the dead faith of the living. Tradition is the living faith of the dead." Which best describes you?

Day Twenty-Eight
Matthew 9:18-26

In today's section, Matthew not only introduces us to new material in Jesus' life, but he also acquaints us with the literary structure known as *intercalation*, a storytelling method that makes purposeful use of interruption in a way that both heightens the narrative tension and highlights new characters. In today's example, Matthew's storyboards in this way: Healing Story Begins, Healing Story Interrupted with Another Healing Story, and Original Healing Story Completes.

In Matthew's case, the Healing/Healing within a Healing/Healing format involves the daughter of a synagogue leader and an unnamed woman suffering from "an issue of blood" (v. 20 DRA). Mark tells the same two stories with the same intercalation format in Mark 5:22–43, another relatively rare example of Mark as wordier than Matthew.

What is the connecting thread of these two interconnected stories? The synagogue! Let me show you what I mean.

As you may or may not know, the religious center of Jewish faith at the time of Jesus was the Jerusalem temple. That's where the sacrificial system described in the book of Leviticus was played out with an array of priests and high priests. Yet when the Jews had been scattered—as in the Assyrian destruction of the Northern Kingdom in 722 BC and the Babylonian exile of the Southern Kingdom of 587 BC—the faithful had to answer this question: "How do we worship God and learn God's Word when we can't assemble in the temple?" The answer was the synagogue, teaching and worship centers established throughout the Mediterranean world. If the focus of the temple was on sacrifice (in many ways it was a religious slaughterhouse), the focus of the synagogue was on teaching.

Well, I know you're grateful for that quick lesson regarding Jewish worship, but what does that have to do with these two intercalated stories? Look at Matthew 9:18: "While he was saying this, a synagogue leader came and knelt before him and said, 'My daughter has just died. But come and put your hand on her, and she will live.'" As the synagogue leader (Mark tells us his name was Jairus), he was responsible for both the physical upkeep of the building and the religious programming that went on within it. In modern terms, he was in charge of both ministry and operations. He has a heavy burden, made heavier by the death of his daughter.

Jesus responds immediately to the man's request: "Jesus got up and went with him, and so did his disciples" (v. 19). While on the way, "a woman who had been subject to bleeding for twelve years came up behind him and touched the edge of his cloak" (v. 20). You've probably heard that phrase also translated as "the hem of his garment." However you word it, most experts think what she touched likely looked like a tassel. The woman herself was no doubt emaciated after suffering for so many years. From the perspective of these two stories, however, here's what you need to know: as one with a continual flow of blood, she was regarded as *unclean*, and everything she touched became unclean. She was unwelcome in the temple or the synagogue.

All of this helps us see the thread that connects these stories. They're about bringing exiles home and outcasts in. Matthew knows what he's doing!

The woman's audacious touch of Jesus' tassel could easily have backfired on her. Remember: everything she touches became unclean, in the ancient mind. Yet Jesus makes clean what the world labels unclean, and she receives immediate healing. "Take heart," he says. "Your faith has healed you" (v. 22). Her bold, convention-defying faith opened up the pathway for Jesus' immeasurable love. What a story and what a Savior!

Now Jesus can return to his original healing assignment. When he arrives at the home of the synagogue leader, he finds a chaotic scene. In keeping with accepted grief protocols, the home is filled with both people and sound: flute (pipe) players, friends and family wailing, and the closest family rending their garments. Matthew purposely evokes memories from the storm in 8:23–27; can Jesus bring calm where there is chaos?

He can and he does. He corrects the people much as he had rebuked the storm: "Go away. The girl is not dead but asleep" (9:24). The reaction: "But they laughed at him." Like Sarah in the book of Genesis, the crowd will discover it is never wise to laugh at the power of God. Matthew's economy of words is remarkable: "After the crowd had been put outside, he went in and took the girl by the hand, and she got up. News of this spread through all that region" (vv. 25–26).

What kind of man is this? One with authority over the storms, over the demons, over Matthew the author, over sickness, over the synagogue and its exclusionary rules, and now even over death itself.

The interruption in today's story suggests that we sometimes have to wait for God's deliverance . . . yet what God does for us while we wait is as important as what we receive at the end of waiting.

Day Twenty-Nine
Matthew 9:27-38

Today's section pictures Jesus very much on the go: "Jesus went on from there" (9:27), "When he had gone indoors" (v. 28), "While they were going out" (v. 32), "Jesus went through all the towns and villages" (v. 35). All this movement foreshadows the sending out of the Twelve in Matthew 10. In the meantime, just know that none of these subtle details are by accident; they're all contributing to the larger story Matthew is telling.

In the first movement (vv. 27–31), Jesus heals two men who are blind. Note that they call him "Son of David" in verse 27. They understand at some level that he is the Messiah, even if they believe he will be a military leader like his ancestor with the sling. Note also that Jesus does not heal them in the crowds and on the street but instead in privacy after they "had gone indoors" (v. 28). He further asks, "Do you believe that I am able to do this?" The answer is emphatic: "Yes, Lord." Apparently, in the move from the crowded streets to the privacy of a home, the men themselves move from a surface-level understanding of Jesus to a surrendered relationship to him. Jesus rewards their faith with his healing.

Knowing the furor that this miracle will cause and not yet ready to be caught up in the reaction, Jesus commands silence. The men disobey (v. 31). This is a consistent pattern in the Gospel, and upon reflection, it does seem to be an instance of disobedience at which Jesus almost winks and nods, as if to say, "I tell them to keep quiet about me, but they just can't do it." I hope the same is true of us.

The next vignette involves a demon-possessed man who has been rendered mute. Again, the healing is immediate, as "the man who had been mute spoke" (v. 33). The point of this miracle is the reaction to it:

The crowd: "Nothing like this has ever been seen in Israel!" (v. 33)

The Pharisees: "It is by the prince of demons that he drives out demons" (v. 34).

In that contrast we see this truth: neutrality to Jesus is not an option. We respond to him either in wonder or with cynicism. Any move toward neutrality aligns us with cynicism. Lord help us if we trend there.

Propelled by his own miracle-working power, Jesus continues his "on the go" mission in 9:35. Note the threefold purpose: teaching, preaching, and healing. Sounds like recipe for a local church, doesn't it?

What strikes us from this ministry summary is Jesus' attitude toward the people: "he had compassion on them, because they were harassed and helpless" (v. 36). Why were they both harassed and helpless? Because their religious leaders were the Pharisees, the same ones who accused Jesus of being a tool of the devil in driving out the diseases of the devil. I pray that I'll be moved by that same kind of compassion when I see folks deceived by either corrupt religious leadership or, more commonly, the false promises of the social media world.

Jesus is either Lord of everything
or he's not Lord of anything.

Day Thirty
Matthew 10:1-31

Today's section of Scripture is a bit longer. For the bulk of it, I will provide some general thoughts only. However, before we dig in, remember where we have just been in Matthew. Jesus has just unleashed a flurry of miracles, and those miracles engender much opposition and conversation among the religious elite. At the end of it all, he asks his followers to ask the Lord to send out workers into the harvest field (9:38).

In Matthew 10:1–31, it's as if Jesus answers his own prayer. Immediately after asking his followers to ask the Lord to send out workers, Jesus sends out workers! See how much better it is to read the Bible, rather than just reading Bible verses?

Look closely at verses 1–4, where Matthew lists "the Twelve." He first calls them "disciples" (v. 1) and then "apostles" (v. 2). These twelve were called from among a much larger group of people who followed Jesus, and they are given special authority and roles as his leading heralds. These are the men into whom Jesus will pour his own life and to whom he will give the privilege of establishing and distributing the church. What follows in Matthew 10 is almost a *test run* of what they will do after his departure. It's a preliminary version of the book of Acts.

Notice two people in particular on this list: "Matthew the tax collector" (v. 3) and "Simon the Zealot" (v. 4). We've already seen in the story of Matthew's call (9:9–13) that our author subtly inserts a bit of his own memoir into Jesus' biography, and he does so here again. Why is Simon called "the Zealot"? It's not a description of his character or his temperament; it is instead an indication of the political party to which he belonged. The Zealots were those in ancient Israel who advocated (and worked for) the overthrow of Roman rule over the promised land; for many that meant by any means necessary. And what is Matthew's occupation? A tax collector—traitor—for the same Roman government that Simon and his Zealots were trying to overthrow.

What Matthew the author is telling us is this: "I am on the same team with a guy who, under different circumstances, likely would have had me imprisoned or executed for treason." Think about a modern parallel you may be familiar with: the people in Iraq and Afghanistan. After US forces departed, those who served as interpreters or aids for the American military were victims of fierce revenge. That's what Zealots did to people like Matthew.

Yet because of Jesus, that's not what happened. Simon didn't execute Matthew; instead they became coconspirators in the Messiah movement we know as the church.

As you survey Jesus' instructions in the rest of the section, you'll see that following this Messiah guarantees much more opposition than popularity. We are, of course, seeing a rise of that in our day as well. Such opposition can either make us discouraged or help us realize that we're not the first and we likely won't be the last. Worse things have happened to more devoted disciples.

I am choosing that second response. I hope you will too.

Recall someone greatly influential in your life of faith. Today would be a good day to thank that person via note, text, or email.

Day Thirty-One
Matthew 10:32-42

If you have one of those Bibles with the words of Jesus in red, you'll notice that these ten verses finish a rather lengthy speech by Jesus. While it is not the longest such speech—both Matthew 5–7 and John 14–17 are much longer—it is one of the most demanding. It is also one in which the careful reader needs to remember what Jesus is *not* saying in the midst of what he *is* saying.

This speech, continued from yesterday's reading, commissions Jesus' twelve apostles for their ministry of *going out* and, in many ways, foreshadows what will happen to and with the larger church in the book of Acts: opposition, persecution, and martyrdom. That's why this section begins with these forbidding words:

> "Whoever acknowledges me before others, I will also acknowledge before my Father in heaven. But whoever disowns me before others, I will disown before my Father in heaven." (10:32–33)

These are high stakes with serious implications. Many in the twenty-first-century church are tempted to edit the gospel to make it more palatable to the culture that surrounds us; we see this most visibly on teachings about marriage, sex, and the body. Yet cultural capitulation never serves the church well. Those who modify the Word to satisfy the world don't win more converts; instead, they only earn more contempt.

Jesus goes on in verses 34–36 to raise the stakes even higher: "Do not suppose that I have come to bring peace to the earth . . ." Then, quoting from the prophet Micah, he locates where the division will be the most painful: within the nuclear family. Some of you have lived this out; others are in the middle of it right now. It makes me think of the young woman who brought her luggage to her baptism, as her father had told her that if she were baptized into Jesus, she could never come home again. She made a painful choice but the right one.

Jesus then repeats the same idea with a slightly different comparison: "Anyone who loves their father or mother more than me is not worthy of me; anyone who loves their son or daughter more than me is not worthy of me" (vv. 37–38). In the midst of that unsettling language, pay careful attention to what Jesus doesn't say. He never says, "Don't love your parents or your kids." It's a matter of priority. The truth is, once you love Jesus the most, you can love your family the best. Your love for them becomes rooted in your love for him. It prevents your family love from becoming an idol and lets them serve as tools in your overall life of faith.

All of Jesus' statements regarding family dynamics build to the summary statement:

> "Whoever finds their life will lose it, and whoever loses their life for my sake will find it." (v. 39)

This is the sort of upside-down, paradoxical logic that is at the heart of the gospel, a gospel in which the first will be last, the greatest will be servants, and a dead prophet will become a risen Savior. No wonder the world finds the church so offensive! It turns the world's own values upside down and inside out.

When the church modifies the Word to satisfy the world, it doesn't win more converts; it only earns more contempt.

Day Thirty-Two
Matthew 11:1-19

F or reasons I will reveal below, this particular passage has a special meaning for me. and it shows the importance of reading the Bible as opposed to merely reading Bible verses. But before that, a reminder of where we've been. In Matthew 10, Jesus commissioned his apostles to begin the ministry of the church; he also told them the heavy price they will likely pay for following him. His summation is in 10:39: "Whoever finds their life will lose it, and whoever loses their life for my sake will find it." Heavy stuff.

Matthew 11 does little to lighten the mood. The focus reverts to John the Baptist, Jesus' friend and cousin, a man we last saw in chapter 3, when John baptized Jesus. Notice Matthew 11:2–3: "When John, who was in prison, heard about the deeds of the Messiah, he sent his disciples to ask him, 'Are you the one who is to come, or should we expect someone else?'"

Why is John in prison? Aha! Because he called out the Roman ruler, Herod, for divorcing his wife in order to marry his sister-in-law. We often assume we're the first ones to invent sexual scandal; as with most of our modern assumptions, we're off the mark. The imprisonment will ultimately cost John his life. The fact that his disciples ask Jesus a question to which he already knows the answer tells us much about his state of mind. John has known from inside his mother's womb that Jesus is the Messiah. Think I'm strange for saying that? Check Luke 1:39–45, a scene we've called the "in utero leap."

By seeking an answer to a question he's really known since before birth, John is telling Jesus and us: "I'm scared. I'm not sure it's worth it. I don't know if I really want to find my life by losing it." Jesus' awareness of John's failing faith is the source of his answer, as well as one of the more head-scratching verses in Scripture. Jesus begins his response in 11:4–6 with an instruction to John's disciples: Tell John that all the signs of the Messiah are firmly in place—healing, miracles, resurrection, and proclamation.

John's followers get the message and return to their imprisoned leader (v. 7), and then Jesus reminds the crowds of the stature and role of the Baptizer: "Among those born of women there has not risen anyone greater than John the Baptist" (v. 11).

The next verse has caused much confusion and even controversy: "From the days of John the Baptist until now, the kingdom of heaven has been subjected to violence, and violent people have been raiding it" (v. 12). This verse has been translated from the Aramaic (which Jesus spoke) into Greek (which Matthew wrote) and then into English (which we read) in any number of ways. One of the more famous translations is a version used by some of our Catholic friends, which concludes with "the violent bear it away" (DRA).

Some of you may have heard of Flannery O'Connor, an eccentric yet faithful novelist from Georgia in the 1950s and 1960s. One of her best-known novels is *The Violent Bear It Away*. I know this random fact because as an English major in college, I chose her for the subject of my senior thesis.

Novels and novelists aside, what in the world is going on in this verse that seems to glorify violence? Is Jesus saying that the kingdom will be the victim of violence or that violent people will advance it? Many experts from many different backgrounds have interpreted it many different ways. Yet in looking at the best way for us to comprehend it, we need to remember that context is everything. We're not reading a Bible verse; we're reading the Bible! Jesus utters these strange words when talking about his friend and cousin John, whose faith is quickly being replaced by fear. John's proclamation has turned into hesitation.

Jesus knows he needs to *win* John back to faith. John is about to go AWOL on him, and in the battle for the soul of the world, Messiah has to conquer the Baptist before he can conquer sin. John will soon experience the violence that the world offers the kingdom, and so Jesus is aggressive in bringing him back to faith. One way of saying it is this: Jesus has to conquer his friends before he conquers his enemies. As Matthew will detail for us in the material to come, much of Jesus' most painful wrestling will come with those who love him the most: Peter, James, John, and, yes, Judas. It's why Paul devotes so much of his time to addressing battles within the church and so little (as in none) to encouraging the church to fight culture wars.

Today, stop and ask yourself:
"Has Jesus fully conquered me?"

Day Thirty-Three
Matthew 11:20-30

....

Geography continues to matter for Matthew, and since it's important to him, it will be important to us as well. It's a frightening moment for three cities highlighted there: Chorazin, Bethsaida, and Capernaum. In today's reading, Jesus pronounces a series of woes upon those three cities. Why? Because miracles he performed there led not to faith but to indifference: "they did not repent" (11:20).

The word we read in English as "woe" conveys both anger and sadness. When Jesus sees how his miracles lead to a desire for the next magic show rather than faith in him, he is both outraged and downcast. In addition, Jesus' mention of Chorazin gives us pause, as we have no record of a miraculous event there.

The indictments Jesus issues here remind us that *miracle* faith should never be confused with *authentic* faith. If the history of Israel in the Hebrew Scriptures teaches us anything, it's that miracles often produce faith in miracles and not in the God who sends them. Miracles prepare us for the message; we shouldn't enjoy the one without hearing the other.

Jesus moves from the public indictment of verses 20–24 to the private intimacy of verses 25–26. Read those verses out loud. I love the truth that the realities of the kingdom are hidden "from the wise and learned, and revealed" to children. Does God do the hiding? Or does human pride make the wise and learned incapable of seeing and hearing truth? I'd say both are at play.

Matthew 11:27–28 could hardly be more clear in telling us that the Father and the Son are One. Jesus is neither guru nor prophet nor guide; he is God in the flesh and makes that claim in those verses. The reason he can pronounce *woe* on the cities above is because he has the divine power to make judgment happen. Yet this affirmation of his own divinity explains not only the judgment that precedes it but the comfort that follows. Verses 28–30 provide some of the most peaceful words in Scripture:

> "Come to me, all you who are weary and burdened, and I will give you rest. Take my yoke upon you and learn from me, for I am gentle and humble in heart, and you will find rest for your souls. For my yoke is easy and my burden is light."

I suppose a lot of you have read or heard those verses before; perhaps you have experienced them out of context, as stand-alone words on a Hallmark card. They're nice in that setting, but they are revolutionary in their real setting, the one Matthew has created with his narrative. Whatever an *easy* yoke is (a yoke is an instrument used to direct oxen as they work, and *easy* actually means "well fitting"), Jesus' promises can never be separated from an accurate understanding of who he is: Lord of lords and King of kings. That's why he says "Learn from me" in verse 29! Savor how it is that the Creator entered creation only to have it reject him; and yet that rejection ensures the redemption of our souls. When you understand and celebrate that Jesus is not "one of many" but "the One and Only," then life in him really does fit well. Obedience ceases to be a duty and becomes instead a delight.

....

Jesus' promises to provide can never be separated from his position as King.

....

Day Thirty-Four
Matthew 12:1–14

Matthew pivots his story as chapter 12 begins. From here on, the opposition will increase, and the target on Jesus' back will grow ever larger. The religious authorities in Israel and the political leaders from Rome will eventually align in their joint effort to execute their Creator.

The suspicion and the plot begin with the most mundane of activities: "At that time Jesus went through the grainfields on the Sabbath. His disciples were hungry and began to pick some heads of grain and eat them" (12:1). Now: most of you know the commandment that says, "Remember the Sabbath day by keeping it holy" (Exodus 20:8). It's one of the Big Ten and establishes a way for Jews to set apart one day (to be *holy* is to be "set apart") for the purpose of rest. The Sabbath was both a gift from God and a test of faith, for in a subsistence economy no sane person would refrain from work. What you may not know, however, is that while the biblical command is relatively simple and broadly worded, the ancient rabbis crafted a lengthy list of activities they deemed forbidden under Sabbath law. Over time, these extra-biblical lists came to have almost the same level of authority as the Scripture itself. Among the forbidden activities was both harvesting grain and carrying any type of food product.

To be clear in this instance: the disciples were not stealing. Deuteronomy 23:25 says this: "If you enter your neighbor's grainfield, you may pick kernels with your hands, but you must not put a sickle to their standing grain." In a subsistence economy, you may subsist (!) but you must not hoard.

So what the disciples do here is both legal and moral; *when* they do it is the problem in a world where man-made law has the authority of God-given scripture. This explains the Pharisees' objection in Matthew 12:2.

Jesus' answer to that objection comprises verses 3–8. After citing King David, Jesus next makes the rather obvious point in verse 5: "Haven't you read in the Law that the priests on Sabbath duty in the temple desecrate the Sabbath and yet are innocent?" What does that mean? That the priests work on the Sabbath, whether by observing sacrificial ritual or teaching from the Scripture. It's one reason I have to smile whenever Christian pastors get on a Sabbath high horse: Sunday is the most intense day of work for any preacher worth his or her salt.

Jesus also cites Hosea 6:6, "I desire mercy, not sacrifice." In both its original setting and in how Jesus appropriates it, Hosea is a reminder that people are more important than ritual. Helping is greater than observing. Jesus' entire argument builds to yet another moment of divine self-disclosure: "For the Son of Man is Lord of the Sabbath" (Matt. 12:8) That assertion is, in itself, enough to get Jesus killed; no doubt, that's why he makes it.

As if to underscore Jesus' use of Hosea 6:6 ("mercy, not sacrifice"), Jesus' next Sabbath disobedience involves healing a man with a shriveled hand. Jesus' opponents see a chance to trap him further: "Looking for a reason to bring charges against Jesus, they asked him, 'Is it lawful to heal on the Sabbath?" (Matt. 12:10).

Jesus' answer deploys the "from lesser to greater" logic perfectly. He references a law in which it is legal to help an animal out of a pit on the Sabbath and then makes a brilliant if obvious observation: "How much more valuable is a person than a sheep!" (v. 12). As if to prove the point he has just made, he heals the man's hand in verse 13.

I love the response of the Pharisees to Jesus' logic and his miracle, as it's the kind of reaction that continues to this day. Given logic they cannot refute (a person is more valuable than a sheep) and a miracle they cannot deny (a formerly shriveled hand now "as sound as the other"), they resort to rage. Not better logic and not deeper faith, just greater anger: "But the Pharisees went out and plotted how they might kill Jesus" (v. 14).

From this moment on in Matthew, the cross is inevitable. The creation has met its Creator, does not like what it sees, and so resolves to eliminate him. The lengths to which Jesus' adversaries will go and the lies they will tell will become more and more apparent as we go deeper and deeper into this Gospel, as the good news about God inevitably involves some bad news about people.

God allows opposition to grow desperation.

Day Thirty-Five
Matthew 12:15-29

When we left Jesus yesterday, the mood was menacing in response to his healing a man's withered hand on the Sabbath: "the Pharisees went out and plotted how they might kill [him]" (12:14). From this moment on, opposition will only increase, and the cost of following Jesus will only escalate.

Let's look at what Jesus knows in the very next moment: "Aware of this, Jesus withdrew from that place" (v. 15). Aware of what? The plot to kill him! In response to the death threat, Jesus withdraws. He knows that his death is inevitable, and yet he knows it is not yet time. He is perfectly executing his own execution.

Yet even as he withdraws, he cannot escape the crowds who follow him in order to receive healing from him. His command to silence—"He warned them not to tell others about him" (v. 16)—stems from his awareness that it is not yet time for his trial, death, and resurrection.

In verses 17–21, our author continues his pattern of ensuring that his readers understand that Jesus is the fulfillment of everything that was promised to and through the nation Israel. Here the quotation comes from the Hebrew prophet Isaiah, written hundreds of years before Jesus' birth, promising the coming of a Spirit-formed servant.

As if to prove the foreshadowing, "they brought him a demon possessed man who was blind and mute, and Jesus healed him, so that he could both talk and see" (v. 22). Look at the two responses to this act on Jesus' part:

> All the people were astonished and said, "Could this be the Son of David?" (v. 23)

But when the Pharisees heard this, they said, "It is only by Beelzebul, the prince of demons, that this fellow drives out demons." (v. 24)

The contrast between these two lines tells you everything you need to know about the gospel: the people adore it while the religious leaders reject it.

Listen to Matthew's description of what happens next: "Jesus knew their thoughts" (v. 25). Don't skim over that. Jesus knows what no person has ever known before or since, the thoughts of another. In this case, he recognizes the thoughts of an entire collection of religious leaders bent on his destruction. He launches into a lengthy speech that includes a line Abraham Lincoln would use in his losing 1858 campaign for US Senate: "[A] household divided against itself will not stand" (v. 25). In Lincoln's hands, the statement referred to slavery and his ultimate effort to abolish it. From Jesus' mouth, it points out the absurdity of Satan acting against his own self-interest by casting demons out.

As the address continues, Jesus first makes the provocative claim that in him "the kingdom of God has come upon you" (v. 28) and then asks a provocative question: "How can anyone enter a strong man's house and carry off his possessions unless he first ties up the strong man?" (v. 29). The implication is that in his ministry, Jesus has *bound* the strong man Satan and is in the process of reclaiming what the devil has stolen.

In your prayers today, invite God to "bind the strong man"—the accuser known in Scripture as Satan—so that your ministry area may have radical impact for the gospel.

Day Thirty-Six
Matthew 12:30-37

To review: in Matthew 12:15–29, Jesus countered the Pharisees' shocking claim that he was a secret agent of the devil by pointing out that a house divided against itself cannot stand (v. 25) and then giving us a prayer model (sort of) that involves binding the "strong man" (v. 29).

The insult he has endured at the hands of the religious leaders informs much of what he says in today's reading. It begins with this:

> "Whoever is not with me is against me, and whoever does not gather with me scatters." (v. 30)

Jesus does not offer us the option of *neutrality*. He cannot be "a little important" or "kind of inspiring." More to the point, he can't really be "part of my life." He either *is* your life or he's not. That's why Paul, in an aside to top all asides, tells the Colossians, "When Christ, who is your life, appears, then you also will appear with him in glory" (Col. 3:4). Paul knew what Jesus was talking about here.

Jesus raises the stakes higher in Matthew 12:31–32 in speaking of "blasphemy against the [Holy] Spirit" as something that won't be forgiven. How can there be an unforgivable sin? Two things to note: (1) if you're worried about whether or not you have committed it, that means you haven't! People who are in that place against God have been so dulled by lies and sin they no longer feel guilt or responsibility. (2) I believe this blasphemy is less an act you commit and more an attitude you have, to the point that the attitude has you. It's not a moment in time but a journey into spiritual death in which a person ultimately replaces a living Savior with a dead master, even to the point of accusing Jesus of performing his works by the power of evil. That master is sin or self or some combination of the two, and it convinces a person that he or she does not need God. It's a slow descent into eternal death, and I strongly suggest you don't take the first step.

Matthew 12:33–37 is in some ways even more chilling. For those of us who can be both callous and careless with our words, Jesus says this: "For the mouth speaks what the heart is full of" (v. 34).

I don't have much concern that I have committed or will commit "the unpardonable sin." In contrast, I am acutely aware that the words I say to myself and those I share with a few confidants reveal a heart that is several degrees darker than I want to admit. What does your searching and fearless moral inventory of your words reveal? A heart full of optimism and joy or one of cynicism and strife?

Would you like to learn optimism and practice joy today? Then spend the next five minutes writing down all the things in your life for which you are grateful. Don't just think about them; take the time to make a record of them by writing them down.

Day Thirty-Seven
Matthew 12:38–50

A t this stage of the Gospel of Matthew, the author is showing the escalation of opposition to Jesus the Savior. In particular, Jesus' teaching and his miracles have earned the ire of the religious elite of ancient Israel, the Pharisees and teachers of the law.

This explains 12:38: "Then some of the Pharisees and teachers of the law said to him, 'Teacher, we want to see a sign from you.'"

Let's see . . . in just the last few chapters, Jesus has healed a sick woman and raised a dead girl (9:18–26); he has healed two blind men as well as a man who could not speak (9:27–37); and he has restored the withered hand of yet another man (12:9–14). In other words, there has been a pile on of signs!

The request confirms two things I've written: (1) miracles often lead to faith in more miracles rather than faith in the miracle worker; and (2) many people ask questions not because they want an answer but because they want an advantage. Both are true with this request of 12:38, as the religious elite are motivated by the next *magic trick* and by the desire to put Jesus in an uncomfortable situation.

All that explains why Jesus answers their request not with a sign but with a rebuke. In verse 40, he cites Jonah, doing so in a way that foreshadows his own resurrection. But don't miss the heart of his reply in verse 41: "The men of Nineveh will stand up at the judgment with this generation and condemn it; for they repented at the preaching of Jonah." Do you know what the "men of Nineveh" were like? In the time frame of 800–600 BC, they were notorious for the brutality of their warfare, the cruelty of their treatment of vanquished foes, and the wickedness of their pagan worship. That's a trifecta! And Jesus says to religious Jews, "Nineveh? Y'all are a lot worse than they ever were." Why such stinging condemnation? Because Jonah communicated the Lord's truth (albeit reluctantly), and the

Ninevites repented. When Jesus did the same for the Pharisees, they asked for more signs. Jesus' summary: "Now something greater than Jonah is here" (v. 41), an assertion he repeats in comparing himself to Solomon in verse 42. Indeed it is.

In verses 43–45, Jesus draws an odd analogy regarding impure spirits that leave a person and then ultimately return, leaving that same person worse off than before. The key seems to be in verse 44: "it finds the house unoccupied," a state suggesting that although evil has been banished, it was not replaced by good. As any recovering addict can tell you, recovery happens not only when alcohol or drugs are set aside, but when they are replaced with fitness, with community, and with faith. In the same way, a living relationship with Jesus involves not only a no to that which destroys, but a robust yes to all that gives life.

The final paragraph of today's section is at first glance unsettling. Someone in the crowd lets Jesus know that his "mother and brothers" (v. 47) are standing outside, presumably longing to see him. Jesus' answer in verses 48–50 affirms that his *new* family consists of his disciples. Is Jesus dismantling the nuclear family? Are we to take from these words that we place too much emphasis on Mom, Dad, and the kids? Hardly, and don't countenance those who make such a suggestion. We see Jesus' tenderness toward his mother while he hangs on the cross in John 19:25–27, and we know that his brother James became both a church leader and a biblical author. Here, Jesus' answer instead affirms that he is growing an entirely new community with an entirely new purpose, declaring the arrival of the kingdom of God.

Ask yourself honestly: Do I ask questions because I want answers or because I like attention? To gain information or to seize an advantage?

Day Thirty-Eight
Matthew 13:1-23

M atthew 13 is Jesus' parable chapter. By way of comparison, this same material is in Mark 4, which lets you know Matthew tells the same story in much the same order but adds a great deal more detail. Notice again, Jesus has to adjust his approach because of the size of the crowds (v. 2). This time, instead of retreating, he teaches while seated in a boat.

Jesus' first parable is about the sower and the seed (vv. 3–9). Jesus describes four types of seeds: (1) one type is consumed by birds; (2) another type is consumed by the sun; (3) a third seed is consumed by thorns; and (4) a fourth type isn't consumed at all but instead consumes the Word with joy and favor. Jesus then concludes with an intimidating imperative: "Whoever has ears, let them hear" (v. 9).

After providing this analogy to the crowds, his inner circle, "the disciples" (v. 10), ask for a private interpretation. Jesus gives them one, but not before the unsettling words in verses 11–15, where he retweets Isaiah 6:9–10 as well as phrases from Deuteronomy, Jeremiah, and Ezekiel. Check out his explanation:

"Otherwise they might see with their eyes,

　　hear with their ears,

　　understand with their hearts

and turn, and I would heal them." (v. 15b)

Now, that answer goes against the grain of so much we assume, doesn't it? We've always thought that because everyone loves a good story, parables were designed to make the message easier to understand. Yet here he suggests the opposite; they're designed for challenge more than clarity. Why would Jesus do that?

The answer has to do with the crowds that Matthew has been careful to describe. Jesus knows the crowds are growing. They're impressed with the show, and their faith is turning into faith in miracles, not faith in the miracle worker. The parables are designed to separate the serious from the superficial.

If Jesus were still able to make that kind of distinction—serious from superficial—which side would you land on? The way Jesus tells the story, with the "Word-consuming" soil at the end, here's the answer I long for in my life: "Lord, may you be the all-consuming reality for me and in me!"

After those challenging words, Jesus then gives a pretty straightforward interpretation of his parable. I love the clarity of verse 18: "Listen then to what the parable of the sower means." Got that? Jesus does the heavy lifting of interpreting his own parable for us.

The implication, of course, is that he wants those receiving the explanation to be the good soil, not so they'll be *good*, but so they will multiply. When you think about it, those of us today who name Jesus as King do so because we are part of that thirty-, sixty-, one hundred–fold yield that the first disciples produced and Jesus described in verse 23.

If Jesus tells parables to distinguish between the serious and the superficial, in which category would he find you?

Day Thirty-Nine
Matthew 13:24–30, 36–43

Y our reading today jumps past Matthew 24:31–35. That's because we have, today, another intercalation. Jesus tells a story,
then tells two smaller stories, and then explains the first story to
his inner circle. It's this: Wheat and Weeds / Mustard Seed / Yeast /
Wheat and Weeds explained.

We'll look at the bookends today and return to the intercalated
stories in tomorrow's reading: the parables of the mustard seed and
the yeast.

First, notice the formula Jesus introduces for parable telling in
13:24: "The kingdom of heaven is like . . ." How would we define
this kingdom even before exploring Jesus' analogy to it? It's interesting to note that in Matthew, Jesus almost always says "the kingdom
of heaven," while in Mark it is usually "the kingdom of God." Why
the difference? Ah . . . it's the audience! Mark's audience is primarily Gentile and so not offended by the use of the word *God*. As we
have seen from the very beginning, Matthew's intended audience is
heavily Jewish, and Jews in that day and this are reluctant to say the
name *God* out loud.

But back to the defining question: what is this kingdom? It is
not a picture of heaven. When Jesus says, "The kingdom of heaven
is like . . . ," he is not saying, "Here's what it will be like when you
die." Nor is he saying, "Here's what is going on in heaven right now
while you're stuck here on earth." Instead, Jesus conveys something
very particular; planet Earth has been invaded by its Maker, who
ushers in a new reality to all who will become citizens of it. The
kingdom has broken through in the form of its king and in so doing
empowers its citizens to break out of complacency and malaise. It

will be completed at the end of all days, but until that time, it operates subversively on planet Earth. Its citizens are keenly aware of how the kingdom works; the majority of people are oblivious to its truth and its beauty.

This "side-by-side" nature of the kingdom is the point of today's parable. A man sowed good seed in his field (v. 24) but then, "while everyone was sleeping" (v. 25), an enemy sowed weeds and went away. This kind of thing actually happened in ancient Israel, so as Jesus was telling his story, no doubt the ancient audience gave knowing nods. In our day, we may say that the kingdom is like a software program loaded onto your hard drive—and then an enemy secretly downloads malware onto your system.

In verses 27–28, the field owner's servants want to pull up the weeds now, but the owner urges patience. Why? Because in uprooting the weeds, some of the good wheat may be damaged. Instead, Jesus says, "Let both grow together until the harvest. At that time, I will tell the harvesters: First collect the weeds and tie them in bundles to be burned; then gather the wheat and bring it into my barn" (v. 30).

What does all that mean?

Well, we don't even have to do a lot of interpretive work, as Jesus does it for us.

Note what happens in Matthew 13:36, after the intercalation of the mustard seed and the yeast: "Then he left the crowd and went into the house. His disciples came to him and said, 'Explain to us the parable of the weeds in the field.'" So Jesus' inner circle gets the private explanation of this parable in the same way they received interpretation of the first parable in this sequence, the parable of the sower (13:1–23). In Jesus' explanation:

The sower of good seed is Jesus. (v. 37)

The field is the world. (v. 38a)

The good seed is the people of the kingdom. (v. 38b)

The weeds are the people who belong to the evil one. (v. 38c).

The enemy is the devil. (v. 39)

Wheat and weeds will grow up side by side, doing so in a way that makes it difficult to tell one from the other, until "the end of the age" (v. 40). When Jesus returns, his messengers will separate wheat from chaff, including this chilling promise: "they will weed out of his kingdom everything that causes sin and all who do evil" (v. 41). Both evil things and sinful people will be excluded, cast into a realm full of "the blazing furnace, where there will be weeping and gnashing of teeth" (v. 42). In contrast, the "righteous will shine like the sun in the kingdom of their Father" (v. 43).

That's pretty clear, isn't it? What do we take from this word that is simultaneously harsh and lovely? Menacing and promising? Three certain takeaways:

1. Within the world of the church, wheat and weeds will appear at the same time, and it is often difficult to tell the difference. In our efforts to *weed out* the church, we might weaken the wheat.

2. Therefore, we ought to monitor ourselves regarding judgmentalism.

3. While we need caution regarding being judgmental, we should always remember: judgment is coming. And God's judgment is never wrong, never unfair. By faith, we opt to be among those who will in fact "shine like the sun in the kingdom" (v. 43) while remembering that "it is a dreadful thing to fall into the hands of the living God" (Heb. 10:31).

On a side note, I try to remember this parable when processing criticism. Even among the most outrageous of accusations, there is almost always a kernel of truth. The key is to embrace the wheat, discard the chaff, and retain your own sense of purpose.

....

Think back to the last time you were criticized. Where is the kernel of truth you're tempted to overlook?

....

Day Forty
Matthew 13:31–35

Yesterday, we looked at the intercalation of the parable of the wheat and the weeds, in which Jesus tells that parable, then tells two more, and then explains the opening analogy. Today, we look at the "two more," the parable of the mustard seed and the parable of the leaven.

The Parable of The Mustard Seed

Seeds are so commonplace that we often forget how remarkable they truly are. An acorn, for example, has within it the capacity to become an oak tree. Its current size is microscopic compared to its potential size. Is there any better analogy to the way the church heralds the kingdom of God? Jesus takes twelve men, sacrifices himself, subtracts one (Judas), and within three hundred years that movement dominates the Mediterranean world. Within two thousand years, it has over 2 billion people around the world who call Jesus "Lord" and live with the designation *Christian*. If you have said yes to Jesus, you are part of the phenomenal yield those first seeds have brought.

The Parable of The Yeast

Warning: this parable is not gluten-free. Instead, Jesus makes an everyday observation—that when a baker adds *fermented* yeast to the dough, the bread transforms. It expands, lifts, and adds texture and flavor.

Hear this: God loves you exactly as you are. No strings. Yet hear this as well: God loves you too much to let you stay exactly as you are. Being loved by God is not the same as being indulged by God.

Divine love isn't always permissive but it is always redemptive. No exceptions.

If the gospel doesn't transform, elevate, lift, and change, it's not the gospel. Jesus wants to *yeast* you today. Let him today, thanking him for the difficult process of growth and change.

Why does Jesus speak in such earthy terms? To fulfill what Psalm 78 had been declaring about him all along: "I will utter things hidden since the creation of the world" (Matt. 13:35; see Ps. 78:2: "I will utter hidden things, things from of old").

If you're being called into full-time, vocational ministry, you can run but you cannot hide. God will win out and pull you in.

Day Forty-One
Matthew 13:44-46

After a chapter full of parables, Jesus winds up this teaching section with a parable couplet—the parables of the hidden treasure and the pearl of great price. These two are more interconnected than any other parable pairing in the Gospels. Understanding them well is a matter of nouns and verbs.

The primary curiosity surrounds the actual subject matter of the stories: Is the kingdom like the man plowing? Or is it the treasure he found? Is it like the merchant? Or the pearl he found? The nouns of treasure and pearl? Or the characters of the farmer and the merchant?

I've come to realize that all these noun-centered conjectures miss the mark. Jesus is not saying that a living relationship with him is like the nouns (treasure, pearl); he is saying it's like the verbs (plowing, discovering). The action! The finding, the selling, the buying! The discovering, the abandoning, the embracing, the surprise, the recklessness, the joy. That's what the two stories have in common. That's why Jesus tells them one right after another. That's why Matthew arranges them this way. The *selling* (verb) hinges on two special words: "all" in verse 44 and "everything" in verse 46.

The two men find something totally unexpected—a generic treasure and a very specific pearl—and both realize that this one new thing requires everything from them. So, they sell everything, not as an act of generosity to give to the poor, but as an act of extreme selfishness that knows it can't let the new thing get away. The nouns here matter only a little bit while the verbs matter a lot!

The kingdom of heaven is like a merchant looking for fine pearls. Not diving for pearls, but searching for them. The merchant was trying to buy an assortment of pearls (unlike the plowman who wasn't looking for anything; he just found it).

Here's another detail that adds texture to the story. How are pearls made? In an oyster, of course. If you are Jewish, what kind of animal is an oyster? Unclean! Not kosher! The beauty may be undeniable, but the origins are unacceptable.

Our shady hero, while depending on other folks to do the dangerous job of pearl diving, finds not *a* pearl but *the* pearl, the essence of pearl-ness. Is it just big? Or perfect? Or bigly perfect? We don't know. All we know is his reaction; he sells all that he has, not to give it to the poor, but to keep the proceeds so he can buy his pearl! That's what he does. You know what that means? He is no longer a merchant; he's a collector. He's no longer a capitalist. He's more like a philanthropist! Finding the treasure altered his actions completely and irrevocably. All, everything.

So where does this antihero leave us? Is he the parallel to the kingdom? Is he the role model for those of us who, when we die, want to leave the realm of earth and enter the kingdom of heaven? Is the pearl the main actor in the story? Guess what? It's those two connector words—*all* and *everything*—where he trades one identity in for another. Here's the conclusion: If Jesus isn't Lord of everything, he's not Lord of anything. That's why Jesus tells these pile-on stories. Most of us are good at compartmentalizing life (this is my work life; this is my home life; this is my recreation life; here is my spiritual life; this is my spouse; here is my fling). We fit life into compartments. Jesus says no to all that. *If I'm not Lord of the whole thing, I'm not Lord of anything.*

> **If you can declutter *your life*, you can de-compartmentalize *it as well. Stop giving Jesus some of it so you can gift him all of it.***

Day Forty-Two

Matthew 13:47-58

....

With this reading, we will bring to a close the great parable section of Matthew's Gospel. Before we look at the closing parable ("The Net") as well as a closing analogy (storehouse), and a closing vignette (a prophet without honor in his hometown), here is a quick summary of Matthew's parables compared to that of the other Gospels.

- Matthew's parables are almost all agricultural in nature (sower, weeds, mustard seed).

- Mark features many of the same parables, just fewer of them and told with more brevity. That's one more reason Mark has sixteen chapters compared to Matthew's twenty-eight.

- Luke's parables are more relational in nature. Only in his Gospel do we find the two best-known and most poignant parables: "the Good Samaritan" and "the Prodigal Son."

- John has no parables. He makes up for it with the I AM sayings. I AM: "the way and the truth and the life" (14:6) "the resurrection and the life" (11:25), "the bread of life" (6:35), and, of course, my favorite given the name of the church I pastor, "the good shepherd" (10:11, 14).

With that, we move to the parable of the "the Net" in verses 47–51. Notice again the familiar phrase "The kingdom of heaven is like . . ." I have heard parables described as God's autobiography, and I concur. Jesus is himself the King ushering in the kingdom of which he speaks and about which he paints. In this case, Jesus uses a fishing trip to tell the same story with the same truth as "the wheat and the weeds" in Matthew 13:24–30. The fishing net catches all kinds of fish, some good and some bad, but the separation happens later.

His point? "This is how it will be at the end of the age" (v. 49a), not at the beginning of the age, not in the middle of it, but only at the end. And who is the agent of this separation? "The angels" (v. 49b), the Lord's appointed messengers will, in some way execute God's judgment when God returns to judge the quick and the dead. Just because judgment is delayed does not mean it is uncertain. Just because judgment is certain does not mean it is our job to carry it out. That job belongs exclusively to God, in God's time, and in God's way.

Jesus asks his disciples (with whom he has been having a private conversation since 13:36), "'Have you understood all these things?' . . . 'Yes,' they replied" (v. 51). Future events will reveal that their confidence is not completely warranted. In the meantime, Jesus concludes his Parable-Palooza with a suggestion that each "teacher of the law" who becomes his disciple "is like the owner of a house who brings out of his storeroom new treasures as well as old" (v. 52). Faith in Jesus, then, does not jettison the faith of Moses; it is built upon its treasures and insights. We should all be wary of teachers who claim a *new truth* that is disconnected from what is ancient and worthy. The gospel is not clay to be molded; it is a treasure to be savored.

The final scene (vv. 53–58) has Jesus return home to Nazareth to preach and teach among the people with whom he had grown up. Did they call it a "homecoming celebration"? Was there a covered dish dinner that followed, to which people brought their best dishes in their finest Tupperware? We're not sure because Matthew doesn't say. What he does say implies that the atmosphere was more skeptical than celebratory. The summary statement of the town's reaction to their local boy made good? "And they took offense at him" (v. 57). Jesus' own summary in response is one of those sayings that has endured with multiple applications to multiple figures in history:

"A prophet is not without honor except in his own town and in his own home" (v. 57). The atmosphere of suspicion leads Jesus to keep his miracle-working power under wraps (v. 58), though that will be short-lived.

Doubt, suspicion, rejection from the people he had grown up loving and admiring; it must have been a challenge. It must have disappointed him. Yet it also served to prepare him for the hard news he'll receive as the parables end and the journey to the cross begins.

God uses rejection and its pain to make you a person of greater depth and faith than you ever could have been without it.

Day Forty-Three
Matthew 14:1–21

Today's reading contains two very different scenes that, at first glance, have little to do with each other and yet deeper reflection shows that they flow together with great purpose. The first is a flashback to John the Baptist's beheading, and the second is what we call the "feeding of the five thousand."

Herod Antipas and John the Baptist

Herod (full name: Herod Antipas) ruled over what is today Israel as a representative of the Roman government. He was a regional governor of a pagan nation oppressing the people of the Holy Land.

Note the interesting literary technique Matthew uses in 14:1–2: "At that time Herod the tetrarch heard the reports about Jesus, and he said to his attendants, 'This is John the Baptist; he has risen from the dead! That is why miraculous powers are at work in him.'"

What's interesting about that? The last time we saw John the Baptist (11:1–14) he wasn't dead; he was merely imprisoned and doubting. At that time, he was the subject of Jesus' curious observation that "the violent bear it away" (v. 12 DRA), which we interpreted to mean that Jesus has to conquer his friends before he conquers his enemies. A first-time reader (or hearer) of the Gospel of Matthew will pause as chapter 14 begins, thinking, "John's dead?" I'm not sure of the purpose of this flashback strategy; however, I do believe this occasion is unique in Matthew's Gospel. Herod's fear that Jesus is a "risen John" forces Matthew to explain just how it is that John died.

Matthew's response to that need for explanation is in verses 3–12. The story shocks any who think the Bible is full of nice people who do sweet things; instead Matthew spares no details regarding the deception, the incest, and even the gore. Many times, we in the twenty-first century think that no one has ever been as immoral as people in the modern era. The truth is that when it comes to evil, there really is nothing new under the sun. We simply have the technology to catalog all our immorality. Herod Antipas had a brother named Herod Philip, and that brother (may we call him HP while we call his brother HA?) had a wife named Herodias. On a visit to Rome, HA seduced his brother's wife and convinced her to leave her husband and marry him. Got that? HA takes HP's wife. The problem is that HA has his own wife back in the governor's mansion in Israel, and he ultimately jettisons that wife in favor of the new one, the one who used to be with his brother. I would love to have seen their extended family Christmas cards.

Well, John the Baptist calls out Herod Antipas' immorality. Repeatedly. In a way, John's public ire seals his own death warrant, and that's why he is in prison in Matthew 11. Sometime between chapters 11 and 14, the gory story involving Herodias' daughter, a young woman sources tell us is named Salome (HA's niece and step-daughter), does a public dance with a sad result you see in verse 11 of today's reading: John's head on a platter.

Two subtle details reveal the heart of the story from Matthew's perspective. In verse 12, John's disciples bury his body, preparing us for what Jesus' disciples will do with his body. In verse 13, Jesus hears the news, takes a boat to escape, and mourns the death of his cousin in private. It's Matthew's way of telling us: "This man who will himself conquer the grave? He has emotions, empathy, and sorrow." That reality makes what happens next all the more stunning.

The Feeding of the Five Thousand

Though Jesus longs to grieve in solitude, his privacy does not last: "Hearing of this, the crowds followed him on foot from the towns" (v. 13). He is soon besieged with people. Can you imagine just wanting space to breathe and yet people will not leave you alone?

Jesus lands the boat, sees the crowd, and continues to feel raw emotions: "he had compassion on them and healed their sick" (v. 13).

The crowd lingers, alarming Jesus' followers because of the remoteness of their location and the relative lack of food: "Send the crowds away, so they can go to the villages and buy themselves some food" (v. 15).

I suspect that part of Jesus wanted to agree with his followers. "Yes, let's send them away and rest," he might have answered. But Jesus doesn't succumb to the pressure of his disciples. Instead, he comes up with a much better idea. Rather than operating from a perspective of scarcity (what we don't have), he operates from the position of abundance (what we do have). And what we do have includes five loaves of bread and two fish, totaling seven pieces of food, and seven is the number of perfection.

Jesus takes the bread and fish (v. 19a), gives thanks for it (v. 19b), breaks the loaves (v. 19c), and then gives them to the disciples to give to the people. Pay attention to the verbs: *take . . . thank . . . break . . . give.*

What does Matthew wants you to notice? As a member of the early church and one who no doubts communes with his fellow believers daily (see Acts 2:42), Matthew is purposeful in evoking memories of the Lord's Supper celebrations. It's as if he doesn't want to make his readers wait for the *official* Last Supper (26:17–25) before letting them know: the spiritual nourishment you receive when you take the bread and drink the cup together matters, and matters eternally.

The food multiplies, the crowds are fed, and by operating from abundance rather than scarcity, Jesus reaps even more abundance, twelve basketfuls of broken pieces (14:20). The seven pieces of food evoke perfection, as seven is the *perfect* number for ancient Jews. The twelve basketsful of leftovers convey completion, as twelve is the same number as the tribes of Israel. Even the math confirms it: this man is the embodiment of God's hope for Israel. He is the perfect completion of the people of God; as we learn in the Gospel of John, he is "the bread of life" (6:35).

Just when John the Baptist's sad demise makes the reader fear things are spinning out of control, Jesus reminds us of who really is on the throne.

Jesus still occupies that throne today. May this day's communication lead to daylong conversations with this King of kings who really is "able to do immeasurably more than all we ask or imagine, according to his power that is at work within us" (Eph. 3:20).

Allow the communication you're starting now to become conversation all day long.

Day Forty-Four
Matthew 14:22-36

In just a moment, we're going to take a look at a story in the Gospel of Matthew where Peter ever-so-briefly walks on water. It's a story a lot of you have at least heard of if you haven't read it. It's also the source of my wife, Julie's, process for evaluating candidates she interviews for a job. If the person is really good: "He's a water walker." If not, you guessed it: "She's no water walker, that's for sure." But before we actually look at the story, let me remind you of Jesus' *name*, his designation in the overall Gospel of Matthew. It's *Immanuel*, which means "God with us." It's given to him in the nativity story at 1:23: "'The virgin will conceive and give birth to a son, and they will call him Immanuel' (which means 'God with us')."

Understanding Jesus' ongoing presence is essential to interpreting this story. In light of that, his absence as the story opens raises our interest:

> Immediately Jesus made the disciples get into the boat and go on ahead of him to the other side, while he dismissed the crowd. After he had dismissed them, he went up on a mountainside by himself to pray. (14:22–23)

This is the one of the few times in Matthew that Jesus, the God with us, is apart from his disciples. Not only does he separate himself from his entourage; he does so forcefully and purposefully. The people hearing and reading Matthew for the first time would have thought, "That's different. All along he has been 'God with us,' and now it's 'God has left us.'" That's what first-time readers and hearers would have thought. But what about the disciples actually in the story? How did they take Jesus' departure? When Jesus made them go, they must have been deeply unsettled that their abiding presence had become a disturbing absence.

Later that night, Jesus was alone when

the boat was already a considerable distance from land, buffeted by the waves because the wind was against it.

Shortly before dawn Jesus went out to them, walking on the lake. When the disciples saw him walking on the lake, they were terrified. "It's a ghost," they said, and cried out in fear. (vv. 24–25)

Whether it's here in the Gospel of Matthew or in your life and mine, isn't it true there's always a storm? Yet into the middle of this particular storm comes Jesus, and he's the original Water Walker, which generates a new level of fear in his followers. It's interesting: the disciples are less fearful of the storm—because they've seen them before—and much more frightened of Jesus, whom they are witnessing do something no one else has ever done. I suppose that's why so many of us are more scared of uncertainty than we are of misery. With that, Jesus attempts to calm them in verse 27: "Jesus immediately said to them: 'Take courage! It is I. Don't be afraid.'"

Notice that Jesus' solution to their fear centers on his identity, not on his power: "It is I." Rather than calming the storm, he reminds the disciples exactly who he is; in doing so he alerts us that whatever miracle follows only serves to further the message he proclaims.

Peter issues a challenge to Jesus: "'Lord, if it's you,' Peter replied, 'tell me to come to you on the water.'" (v. 28)

Now, you're not supposed to test the Lord your God. Remember? But Jesus lets that one slide. Instead, he allows Peter to put him to the test in 14:29a: "Come," he says.

Matthew wants us to know that Peter the man is a perpetual motion machine. Well, look how 14:29b says it: "Then Peter got down out of the boat, walked on the water and came toward Jesus." Matthew's use of motion verbs is masterful. In consecutive order: "got down," "walked on," and "came toward Jesus." Our author's use of language, word choice, and repetition memorably conveys a constantly kinetic character!

Notice where Jesus is during the water walking. He is no longer with Peter. He is in front of Peter! God with Us is suddenly the Messiah in Front of Us. I can't help but think that's where we most often find God, not by our sides, in our pockets. Instead, God is way ahead of us, beckoning us with that simple "Come." It makes sense now why Jesus left his disciples at the beginning of the story. He had to! He had to leave them alone in order to move ahead of them!

With such a breathtaking triumph on the part of Peter, it seems the story will conclude on a note of victory, an homage to a singular achievement. Yet he undermines all that has come before it: "But when he saw the wind, he was afraid and, beginning to sink, cried out, 'Lord, save me!'" (v. 30).

How do you *see* wind? Matthew doesn't tell us how, but that's apparently what Peter does. Verse 30 is the part of the story most people remember; Peter failed because he took his eyes off his Savior and put them on his situation. But you know what is more true? The eleven who remained on the boat were contained by their fear. Eleven huddled. One leaped! Eleven stayed in place. Only one moved, which means that only one came toward Jesus.

To get close to Jesus, you have to risk something for Jesus.

Your risk will likely hurl you into some kind of chaos; only in radical dependence can you overcome it. Overcoming comes not through skill or strength but through trust. The best thing about our lives is our utter dependence on Jesus; if he has to push us out of the boat and onto the water to get us there, he'll do it.

> *To get close to Jesus, you need to risk something*
> *for Jesus.*

Day Forty-Five
Matthew 15:1-20

As you read Matthew 15:1–20, the scribes and Pharisees are asking why Jesus' followers don't wash their hands before they eat. You may get some déjà vu: "Didn't we recently have an incident just like this?" Yes, we did. It dealt with picking grain on the Sabbath (12:1–2) rather than clean hands. Matthew is arranging his material and escalating the conflict so that in ways large and small, his readers are getting prepared for the end result of the conflicting worldviews held by Jesus and the religious elite—the cross.

In this case, the leaders' question hearkens back to an elaborate system of handwashing that observant Jews had devised. Any modern hand-sanitation instructions are just a fraction of what ancient Jews were supposed to do, as the religious leaders gave commands involving the angle of your forearm, the direction of your fingers, and the volume of water. It was comprehensive cleaning!

All that is behind the accusations hurled at Jesus as Matthew 15 opens. I love how Jesus does not cede any territory in answering: "And why do you break the command of God for the sake of your tradition?" (v. 3). He then reminds the scribes and the Pharisees of the biblical command about honoring parents (v. 4), a command that speaks to caring for them in their old age even more than it directs us to obey them when we're children! And how have the religious elite nullified the biblical command for their own benefit? Money. The scribes and Pharisees told congregants that if they gave so much money to the temple that they were unable to care for Mom and Dad, then it's no sin. The cause of temple maintenance took priority over the command of parental respect. Jesus' assessment of that logic? "Thus you nullify the word of God for the sake of your tradition" (v. 6). And, we might add, for the sake of your own pockets.

What Jesus does next is so interesting. Remember that through-out this Gospel, Jesus is the fulfillment of all that is Israel? It's why one of Matthew's signature phrases is "so was fulfilled . . . ," fol-lowed by an Old Testament quotation. Jesus now uses the strategy in reverse. In verses 8–9, he accuses the Pharisees of fulfilling Isaiah's prophecy (Isa. 29:13): "These people honor me with their lips, / but their hearts are far from me. / They worship me in vain; / their teach-ings are merely human rules." Whoa. That's a prophecy you don't want to fulfill!

Then Jesus became more aggressive in verse 10: "Jesus called the crowd to him and said . . ." What had been a private conflict turns into a public rebuke. How so? The clean/unclean dilemma is less a matter of what you touch or what you eat and more a matter of what is already inside: "but what comes out of their mouth, that is what defiles them" (v. 11).

I love what happens next. The conversation returns to a more in-timate sphere. It's no longer Jesus versus the Pharisees or Jesus among the crowds; instead, "the disciples came to him and asked, 'Do you know that the Pharisees were offended when they heard this?'" (v. 12). Of course Jesus knows this. That was his intention! He's not one to allow empathy to triumph over truth. Some people actually need to get their feelings hurt, particularly if they obscure revealed truth with human invention.

Peter then asks, "Explain the parable to us" (v. 15). "Are you still so dull?" comes Jesus' not-very-kind reply (v. 16), and part of me wants that rebuke to be because he hasn't just told a *parable* but instead made an observation! Nevertheless, Jesus does not then detour into an explanation of the difference between a parable and an observation (I'm such a know-it-all that that's what I would have done) but instead moves to the heart of the matter. Our status as clean or unclean, defiled or holy, is not a matter of what we ingest. It is instead a matter of where our minds rest.

In that regard, you're off to a good start by beginning your day in the Word and not the world. Let this morning communication turn into daylong conversation . . . and don't forget to wash your hands!

By God's grace, you can, in fact, govern where your mind rests. Invite God to heal you of the fixation on the negative and destructive and to give you a focus on the hopeful and purposeful.

Day Forty-Six
Matthew 15:21-28

Matthew 15:21 opens this section with our author's ongoing interest in geography: "Leaving that place, Jesus withdrew to the region of Tyre and Sidon." That means he traveled north and west, out of Galilee, toward the Mediterranean Sea and, more ominously, into Gentile territory. Today, that region is part of the nation of Lebanon.

Why does Jesus *withdraw* to a place where, as a Jew, he could expect to receive hostility? Matthew does not tell us the Messiah's motivation, leaving us with little more than conjecture. Perhaps he needed to rest before what would become the final push into Jerusalem and onto the cross. Or possibly, this excursion foreshadows how the Gospel will conclude, with the command to take the message to "all nations," all people groups and ethnic types (28:19).

While in Tyre and Sidon, "a Canaanite woman from that vicinity came to him, crying out, 'Lord, Son of David, have mercy on me! My daughter is demon-possessed and suffering terribly" (15:22). The descriptor, "a Canaanite woman," is loaded with meaning. From the days of Joshua's conquest (see the book of Joshua, sixth book of the Old Testament, which tells how Israel inhabits the promised land, which is Canaan), Canaanites and Jews have been at odds. They were people of different customs, different values, and different gods; the Canaanites tended to be polytheists, while Jews were, nominally at least, monotheists. That fact makes the woman's declaration all the more remarkable: "Lord, Son of David." Matthew wants us to note that she has faith in the Messiah that the scribes and Pharisees lack.

Jesus' disciples reveal their lingering ethnic animosity in verse 23: "Send her away, for she keeps crying out after us." Matthew follows that slur with a troubling back-and-forth involving this woman and Jesus:

"He answered, 'I was sent only to the lost sheep of Israel.' The woman came and knelt before him. 'Lord, help me!' she said. He replied, 'It is not right to take the children's bread and toss it to the dogs'" (vv. 24–26).

Wait. Is Jesus calling her a dog? Is he being both racist (anti-Canaanite) and misogynist (anti-woman)? Has he succumbed to the worst of the culture in which he was raised and, in so doing, issued an almost unspeakable slur?

Sadly, some contemporary Bible *experts* have said just that. Remarkably those claiming we need to acknowledge Jesus' racial and gender biases have found their way into online platforms or even church leadership, as if they're smarter and more enlightened than Christians who have read this story for two thousand years before them. As you might suspect, I don't agree with those interpreters or that interpretation.

Instead, it is wise to see how the woman took Jesus' words, as a challenge to the absurdity of the divisions between peoples and groups. She responds with both wit and wisdom, not hearing an insult but instead seizing an opportunity: "'Yes it is, Lord,' she said. 'Even the dogs eat the crumbs that fall from their master's table'" (v. 27). What moxie! "Oh, I'll see your sly comment, Jesus, and raise you one better!" The result is that neither falls victim to the ethnic divisions their world (and even the disciples!) would impose upon them; instead, they transform them. "Woman, you have great faith! Your request is granted" (v. 28).

Matthew is Jewish. From the opening words of his Gospel, he has been clear that Jesus is the hope of Israel. And yet the hero of this little encounter is the sworn enemy of the Jews, a Canaanite woman. Far from reinforcing divisions, this story demolishes them.

....
Divisions get demolished and enemies become heroes when Jesus is Lord of all.
....

Day Forty-Seven
Matthew 15:29-39

A s you read today's passage, you're excused for thinking, "Wait—didn't we just do this?" And you'd be right, mostly. Back in 14:13–21, Jesus fed five thousand in the aftermath of the beheading of John the Baptist. Here, in 15:29–39, he feeds four thousand following the healing of the Canaanite woman.

We'll note some similarities and then a startling difference.

Similarities

Jesus withdraws from crowds to a remote area	14:13	15:29
Jesus is followed by great crowds	14:13b	15:30a
Jesus heals the sick the crowd brings with them	14:14	15:30b
Concern expressed for the hunger of the people	14:15 (the disciples)	15:32 (Jesus)
Jesus' motivation is compassion	14:14	15:32
The amount of food available is both numbered and small	14:17 (5 loaves, 2 fish)	15:34 (7 loaves, a few small fish)
Jesus commands the people to sit on the ground (an odd detail to put in both!)	14:19	15:35
Jesus takes, gives thanks, breaks, and gives	14:19	15:36
Jesus multiplies the food almost offstage; mentioned only subtly	14:20	15:37
They all ate and were satisfied	14:20	15:37a
The amount left over suggests something about God's perfection and Israel's completion	14:20 (12 basketfuls)	15:37 (7 basketfuls)

The amount of overlap has led some Bible scholars to suggest that this is the same event described in two slightly different ways. While there is some appeal to that understanding, I believe it ultimately falls short, primarily because of the signature difference between the two miracles.

And the difference has to do with the combination of geography and ethnicity. In Matthew 14, where Jesus feeds five thousand, he is in the region near his hometown of Nazareth (13:53–58). In other words, he is firmly in Jewish territory, ministering to his own people and tribe.

In today's account, Jesus has just left Tyre and Sidon (15:21) and remains on the northern side of the Sea of Galilee. In other words, he is in an area filled with both Jews and Gentiles; monotheists and polytheists; *clean* and *unclean*. This explains the praise he receives in verse 31: "and they praised the God of Israel." The Gentiles are amazed that Israel's God has power in mixed territory and that God's Messiah will touch and love them as well. Jesus healed and fed people with whom the religious elite of Israel would not associate.

Here we have a clear picture of the boundary-breaking, truth-sharing, and gospel-reconciling ministry of Jesus. Feeding the five thousand in Matthew 14 reminds us that his first mission is to "the lost sheep of Israel" (Matt. 10:6; 15:24). Feeding the four thousand in Matthew 15 prepares us for the command that will conclude Matthew's masterpiece: Go and make disciples of *all nations* (Matt. 28:19).

Jesus' feeding miracles prepare us for what's more and what's next. For what is he preparing you today? For whom is he preparing you?

Day Forty-Eight
Matthew 16:1–12

Look at how Matthew 16 starts: "The Pharisees and Sadducees came to Jesus and tested him by asking him to show them a sign from heaven."

Oops. Matthew did it again.

As we saw earlier in this study, the same kind of people asked the same type of question of Jesus in 12:38; although there, instead of the Sadducees alongside the Pharisees, it was "teachers of the law," also known as the scribes. Believe it or not, that's a distinction with a difference.

The Pharisees were a teaching sect within ancient Judaism who emphasized not only the written law of Moses but also the oral law and traditions that rabbis throughout the centuries had added to it. They were "jot and tittle" kinds of people who also believed in both angels and the resurrection of the dead.

The Sadducees were another teaching sect within ancient Judaism who leaned toward wealth and influence and who were content under Roman occupation. They did not believe in the resurrection of the dead, in part because they had lives of privilege in the here and now. If you cuddle up with the occupying force, you receive better treatment than those who resist.

These two unlikely allies test Jesus. Nothing makes for faster friends than a common enemy, and Jesus is that enemy. The test reminds us that some people ask questions, not because they want an answer, but because they want an advantage. That's what's going on here. Jesus knows this, and that's why he gives them a brief lecture on meteorology (vv. 2–3) and then the ultimate *gotcha*: "none will be given [this generation] except the sign of Jonah" (v. 4).

Which is precisely how he answered the previous test, in 12:39–45. By the "sign of Jonah," Jesus is declaring one thing while preparing for another. The declaration? "Just as Jonah was the sign to the Ninevites, so I am the sign to you. I don't need to provide another sign since you're looking at the best evidence of God's invasion of planet Earth that you'll ever see." The preparation? "That three-days-in-the-depths thing? Get ready. It's fixin' to happen again, and nothing will be the same after that." Matthew is a genius, and Jesus is glorious.

In 16:5–12, the conversion shifts because the audience does. Rather than being under attack from the religious elite, Jesus is cross-training with his own cadre of supporters. I love the wit of verse 5: "the disciples forgot to take bread." I think they could be forgiven for this gluten oversight, since Jesus has twice proven he can make a lot out of very little! Yet Jesus takes this opportunity to teach them something specific: "Be on your guard against the yeast of the Pharisees and Sadducees" (v. 6).

In a response more typical of the Gospel of John than of Matthew, the disciples take Jesus literally—"It is because we didn't bring any bread!" (v. 7)—prompting Jesus to explain his own analogy.

The ancient Jews frequently used the term *yeast* to refer to something that has an evil influence in a larger sphere. In the same way that yeast ferments and thus gives *rise* to bread, the Jews felt that evil influence would infect religious teaching to the extent it spoiled what was originally holy. This is what the Pharisees and Sadducees have done with the pure teaching of Moses and the other authors of the Hebrew Bible. They have added to it, twisted it to suit their own needs, and made profane what God designed to be pure.

Specifically, the Pharisees have valued rules over people, while the Sadducees have prioritized political comfort over spiritual truth. In addition, the Sadducees have so domesticated God that they deny the resurrection of the dead, a teaching Jesus will rebuke in dramatic form at the end of Matthew's Gospel.

One group values rules over people. The other prioritizes political comfort over spiritual truth. Some things never change.

With the opposition lined up against him, Jesus needs to make sure his own posse is as prepared as possible for what's to come.

**The gospel always values people over rules
and truth over comfort.**

Day Forty-Nine
Matthew 16:13-20

What is the first rule of real estate? Location, location, location. Where you buy a house or build an office park is more important than the kind of house or park you get. It's all about where a particular structure is located. That's why a bungalow in the elite part of town can go for seven figures while a larger home in a humbler neighborhood costs substantially less. Location, location, location.

I mention that first rule of real estate because nowhere is it more true in Scripture than with a verse in today's reading, Matthew 16:18, where Jesus says to one of his disciples, "I tell you that you are Peter, and on this rock I will build my church, and the gates of Hades will not overcome it." And it turns out that *where* Jesus said this is just as important as *what* he said. Location, location, location. So where is Jesus when he utters these words? Remember: we have been discovering together how context is everything. In this case, the context is not merely literary; it's geographical.

Verse 13 tells us where Jesus was when he spoke with his disciples: Caesarea Philippi. So what's the big deal with that place? What does it have to do with the story? Only everything. Caesarea Philippi was located about twenty-five miles north of the Sea of Galilee, close to where Jesus spent most of his time teaching, healing, and working miracles. It was located at the base of a mountain called Mount Hermon. Caesarea Philippi was, for lack of a better term, a hot zone for idol worship. Even before it was a Roman city, that place had been a religious site dedicated to the worship of other gods for hundreds of years, going back way before the time of Jesus.

Long before the first century AD, the area was not called Caesarea Philippi. It was originally inhabited by some of the Canaanite people, Israel's neighbors who are mentioned throughout the Old Testament. The Canaanites worshiped a god called Baal, who was a well-known storm god at that time. If you read the Old Testament, especially the books of 1 and 2 Kings, you will find that the Israelites were often tempted to worship Baal themselves. This was, of course, a clear violation of the first of the Ten Commandments, where God commands Israel, "You shall have no other gods before me" (Exod. 20:3). But frequently, the people of Israel wanted to hedge their bets and cover their bases in the event that the Lord didn't come through for them. They would worship the Lord, but then go ahead and worship Baal too. They kept Baal in their hip pocket, you know, *just in case.*

The Canaanites, meanwhile, had long believed that Baal was the god of storms, and so in their minds he was responsible for the seasonal cycles of rain, new life, and fertility—the fertility of flora, fauna, and, yes, people. You could say that Baal was the rain-making sex god of the Canaanite people, and the Israelites were tempted to worship him from the moment of their first interactions with their new neighbors. Twice in the Old Testament, Mount Hermon is referred to as Baal Hermon, showing how closely that god was identified with that region (Judg. 3:3; 1 Chr. 5:23). What should have been *terra non grata* for observant Jews instead became a temptation too enticing to resist.

Much later, this territory came under control of the Greeks, who worshiped the god Pan, among others. Traditionally, Pan was worshiped at natural sites, such as caves or springs, rather than in temples. Now, here's another significant fact about the site that eventually became Caesarea Philippi; it was located at the base of sheer, rocky walls containing caves and a natural spring. With the arrival of the Greeks, this spring became an important site for the worship of Pan; the Greeks even called the spring Paneas in honor of their god's name. Pan had much in common with Baal beyond the fact that both were worshiped in this region. Like Baal, Pan was associated with fertility and the renewal of spring. In many ways, Pan is the reincarnation of Baal, just given a different name by different people. And one other critical note about Baal and Pan: the locals believed they hibernated in the Caesarean caves during the winter months and then emerged from them—full of reproductive desire—when the spring warmth began. Spring fever, indeed.

Pan's association with fertility contained an added dimension. He was also a god of sexuality. The worship of Pan at the mouths of these caves involved human acts of fertility and sexuality. Promiscuity. Going to the "church of Pan" meant that you drank all the alcohol you could while sleeping with as many partners as possible, all to honor their god! I don't care how good your praise band or teaching programs are, it is hard for any church to compete against that sort of thing for attention! All this was in and around Caesarea Philippi; it was not only a hot zone for idols but also a red-light district for people.

Now fast-forward to Jesus' own day. After the Greeks came the Romans, who conquered the area and established their own government. The Romans ruled during the time of Jesus. Herod, Pilate, and other names you've heard were proxy rulers for Rome and stationed in Judea. One of those proxy Roman rulers gave our city its name. Herod Philip wanted to honor the emperor, Caesar Augustus, so he named the city Caesarea. Later it came to be known as Caesarea Philippi, after Philip, because other Roman cities were also named Caesarea. It turns out that kissing up to the emperor was a popular thing to do! The Roman rulers claimed supreme authority and even divinity. They too were to be worshiped as gods. Calling the city Caesarea was appropriate for Herod Philip. It was a way to acknowledge the Roman identity of the city and its inhabitants, as well as the lordship of Caesar, who ruled all of Rome's territory. This was the kind of city where you had an ongoing loyalty oath: Caesar is Lord. Caesar's power loomed large at Caesarea Philippi.

All of a sudden, it mattered quite a bit that Jesus is here in Caesarea Philippi when he speaks to Peter and his other disciples. Against this backdrop of idol worship, prostitution, and Caesar's power, Jesus stands up and presses his followers about his own identity. It's as if he invites them to comparison shop and see that there is no comparison at all. Through where he is—location, location, location—this mere Jewish carpenter deliberately sets himself up against all the religions and powers of the world. He asks his disciples, "Who do people say the Son of Man is?" (v. 13). They give the usual answers they've been hearing: John the Baptist, Elijah, Jeremiah, or one of the prophets. But Jesus pushes the issue, wanting them to answer for themselves: "Who do you say I am?" (v. 15).

That's when Simon Peter makes his bold declaration: "You are the Messiah, the Son of the living God" (v. 16). In the shadow of a rock face wall, the one whose name means *rock* steps up, saying that Jesus is the Messiah they've all been waiting for. In the very place where other gods have been said to hibernate in the winter and emerge in the spring—dead gods—Peter says that Jesus is the Son of the living God. In a place named after Caesar, Peter declares that Jesus, not Rome's ruler, is Lord. Peter makes this declaration for the first time here, at Caesarea Philippi, surrounded by the false teachings of sexual immorality, hibernating gods, and Caesar's absolute power. It is at this place, in a moment of courage and clarity, that Peter declares truth in the midst of lies: Jesus is the Son of the living God. Jesus is the Christ, the Messiah. Jesus is Lord, and there is no other. Location, location, location indeed.

Truth and Apathy

I look at the landscape of Peter's descendants in the modern church, and I realize that almost all of its limitations come from that toxic brew of apathy, indecision, and even boredom. The gates of Hades do whatever they can to keep us bound up in these limitations. And yet Jesus tells Peter, the other disciples, and us that these gates of Hades will not overcome the gathering of his people. What is the source of his confidence?

The answer is truth! The answer is to celebrate the truth that Jesus is Lord. Caesar (or our equivalent in today's world) is not Lord; sex is not Lord; idols are not Lord. Jesus, and Jesus alone, is the Son of the living God. Delight in that truth, and it will truly set you free. It will make you come alive inside like nothing else can. That is the source of your enthusiasm, your commitment to Christ and the church. Programs and spectacular worship won't do it, no matter how powerful the music, preaching, or prayers. God help me if I ever get bored with proclaiming and explaining the truth that God became a man and defeated the powers of death. God help me if I ever just read that out of a book matter-of-factly and explain it as dry as toast.

Jesus is Lord, and there is no other.

Day Fifty
Matthew 16:21-28

Yesterday's reading represented a dramatic turning point in the Gospel of Matthew, as Peter became the first human being to understand and declare, "You are the Messiah, the Son of the living God" (16:16). In turn, Jesus promised that upon Peter and his affirmation he would build his church.

What is that aftermath of that great moment? With Peter riding high, on top of the world, looking down on creation, you'd think a celebration is in order, right? Wrong.

Instead, in a rapid reversal, Peter goes from apex to nadir in the blink of an eye. The story shows us not only how precarious is human understanding of divine purpose, but also the Bible's courage in exposing the flaws of its heroes.

Matthew sets it up this way: "From that time on Jesus began to explain to his disciples that he must go to Jerusalem and suffer many things at the hands of the elders, the chief priests and the teachers of the law, and that he must be killed and on the third day be raised to life" (v. 21). It seems a straightforward method of preparing his inner circle for what's to come, doesn't it?

This only makes sense to us who read the story now because we know how the plot plays out. To the characters in the story—Peter, James, John, and the rest of the Twelve—what Jesus says makes no sense. If he is the Messiah, the very hope of Israel, then he would no doubt deliver the Jews from the occupying force of Rome. From this pagan *hot zone* of Caesarea Philippi, Jesus' disciples believe that he should leverage his considerable influence and his remarkable power to overthrow the Gentile rulers who were oppressing God's chosen family. That's the kind of Savior that Peter not only wanted but expected.

He tells Jesus as much in verse 22: "Never, Lord! . . . This shall never happen to you!"

Jesus' rebuke is immediate and emphatic: "Get behind me, Satan! You are a stumbling block to me; you do not have in mind the concerns of God, but merely human concerns" (v. 23).

Did Jesus just call Peter *Satan*? Is the one who is the first to identify Jesus for who he is now also the first one to abandon the faith? What does such a sharp correction say to readers throughout the centuries?

Jesus' words here in Matthew 16 take us back to Matthew 4:1–11 and the temptation in the wilderness. What was the nature of the way Satan tempted Jesus? By offering him power, prestige, influence, and comfort. In other words, what Peter shouts—"This shall never happen to you!"—is the same thing Satan whispers to him all along! When an ally takes on the tempter's tactics, the correction must be forceful. I suspect Jesus' words are as much in exasperation to Satan as they are in frustration with Peter.

The difference? Satan would never "get behind" Jesus. Peter will. Yes, Peter will. Will you?

When you "get behind" Jesus and assume a teachable position, you're in for a season of challenge. The invasion of his kingdom into our world renders meaningless all our definitions of success and happiness. Instead, he offers a way of life in which the values of the world are turned upon their heads. Up is down; down is up; winning is losing; dying is living. The paradox is the point:

> "For whoever wants to save their life will lose it, but whoever loses their life for me will find it. What good will it be for someone to gain the whole world, yet forfeit their soul?" (vv. 25–26)

Those words are well worth memorizing.

One of my friends from church told me recently that he endures whatever life throws at him with that recognition that "to die is gain"

(Phil. 1:21). If the greatest harm your greatest enemy can impose upon you is death, and you know that death brings you into glory, what can the world do to you or take from you that really matters? Nothing. Hallelujah, nothing.

This is the kind of Messiah Jesus will be. Not a military victor but a soul saver.

Jesus invites followers who follow his agenda rather than setting their own.

Day Fifty-One
Matthew 17:1–13

What a privilege we have today! We get to look over the collective shoulders of Peter, James, and John as they experience the incomparable honor of seeing Jesus transfigured before their very eyes. What in the world does that even mean? Stay with me, and we'll find out together.

Look how this scene begins: "After six days . . ." (17:1). Six days after what? Ah! Six days after Peter's thrill of victory followed by his agony of defeat! The victory of being the first human to identify Jesus for who he is, "the Messiah, the Son of the living God" (16:16). During this section of Scripture, time has slowed down. This scene happens neither *immediately* nor *at once* but six days later.

After those six days, Jesus takes the inner circle of his inner circle—Peter, James, and John—to a "high mountain" where "he was transfigured before them" (v. 1b–2a). Notice the descriptions: "His face shone like the sun, and his clothes became as white as the light" (v. 2b). It's a reminder of what Paul later tells us in 1 Timothy 6:16: "[he] lives in unapproachable light." Jesus turns inside out, and the three men get to see it happen before their eyes.

Much is made of the appearance of Elijah and Moses in verse 3. "That's connecting Jesus to the law (Moses) and the prophets (Elijah)," people will say. That's one way to look at the story. Or you might have heard another view expressed in this way: "The fact that Peter wants to build booths and Jesus refuses tells us we can't stay in our mountaintop experiences." Again, there's room for that in our understanding of the story.

Speculating on the role of Moses and Elijah as well as the purpose of the booths largely misses the point, however, which is first in verse 5—"This is my Son, whom I love; with him I am well pleased.

Listen to him!"—and then more dramatically in verse 8: "When they looked up, they no saw no one except Jesus." The reason Moses and Elijah appear is so they can disappear! They get on the stage so they can quickly exit the stage and leave Jesus at center stage! Moses and Elijah are godly, but this story reveals that Jesus is God.

The brief moment of comparison with Jesus, Moses, and Elijah is to demonstrate there is *no comparison*. The other two are great men; Jesus is the enfleshment of our great God.

Jesus doesn't stand among godly men. He reigns alone as Lord of all.

Jesus isn't godly. He is God.

Day Fifty-Two
Matthew 17:14-23

As we open today's reading, Jesus has just been transfigured (17:1–13), a vivid scene that depicts how he is not just godly (like Moses and Elijah), but that he is God. He stands alone, and the disciples stand amazed.

The glow upon Jesus, Peter, James, and John quickly dissipates as they descend the mountain, however, as a man brings his seizure-ridden son to be delivered from a demonic power. While the four have been on the mountain, the other nine disciples have been unable to heal the boy: "I brought him to your disciples, but they could not heal him" (v. 16).

Jesus' words seem unusually harsh: "You unbelieving and perverse generation. . . . How long shall I put up with you?" (v. 17). Is he speaking directly of the nine disciples who failed to heal or to the larger generation inhabiting Israel? It's hard to say for certain, though, as we will see, Jesus uses this encounter as a training moment for his inner circle of trusted followers.

What do they need to learn from it? Perhaps the answer to their question in verse 19: "Why couldn't we drive it out?" Jesus' answer in verses 20–21 is both thrilling to hear and easy to misconstrue:

"Because you have so little faith. Truly I tell you, if you have faith as small as a mustard seed you can say to this mountain, 'Move from here to there,' and it will move. Nothing will be impossible for you."

In the Judaism of Jesus' time, there was a common phrase that went something like this: A great teacher who could interpret and apply Scripture well was said to be an uprooter or pulverizer of mountains. If a teacher could resolve difficulties within the biblical text and makes its meaning clear, then he "moved mountains." Jesus is here using exaggeration to make a point: "If you have faith, then you can overcome difficulties, remove obstacles, and live out my word."

This is what gets me in our cultural moment; Jesus is talking about neither "faith in faith" nor "faith in yourself." Whenever I see motivational segments on athletes today, the line "believe in yourself" is front and center. "Just believe in yourself." While you can't have athletic success without some self-confidence, we should never mistake "believe in yourself" with what Jesus is saying here. It's faith in him. It's believing in him comprehensively, not as an add-on to life, but as life itself.

He suggests as much with his next word to the disciples in verses 22–23, where he predicts his suffering, death, and resurrection yet again and as a result "the disciples were filled with grief" (v. 23).

That's faith, not just when things go well, but when confronted with the reality of life and its inevitable disappointments. When you trust God to take you *through* heartache rather than always guide you *around* it, that is faith that will move mountains in your life and mine.

When you are honest about the doubt you have, God is faithful with the grace he gives.

Day Fifty-Three
Matthew 17:24-27

Because I don't want you to rush through either your reading of Matthew or this guide that accompanies it, today's reading is brief. Yet don't mistake its brevity for insignificance. As is his way, Jesus loads up meaning and transformation in the most random of encounters.

Notice where Matthew moves the action: "After Jesus and his disciples arrived in Capernaum [from Galilee in 17:22], the collectors of the two drachma temple tax came to Peter and asked, 'Doesn't your teacher pay the temple tax?'"(v. 24).

The disciples and Jesus are back in Capernaum, the town to which Jesus moved after he went out on his own and left the family back in Nazareth. What is this temple tax? Well, consider what you know about the Jerusalem temple.

1. Animals had to be sacrificed daily. Each animal had to be fed before being slaughtered. The livestock fees alone made it an expensive place to run.

2. The priests in charge also had to offer wine, flour, and oil to the Lord, along with the sacrificial lambs, goats, and bulls. Those materials were also quite costly.

3. Priests had to dress the part! They had priestly robes, matching head gear, and costly accessories.

Because of the expense of running the temple operation and based loosely on Exodus 30:13, ancient Jews enacted a regulation that every Jewish male over twenty years of age had to pay a temple tax.

In Matthew 17, the "collectors" of the temple tax (not an enviable job, if you ask me) attempt to trap Jesus in the most passive-aggressive of ways, by asking his followers a question they're too scared to ask him directly: "Doesn't your teacher pay the temple tax?" Peter answers (of course it's Peter who leaps to answer first!), "'Yes, he does,'" and then returns to "the house" (v. 25a). Whose house? It could be Peter's mother-in-law's house (8:14–15) or Jesus' own bachelor pad. Matthew does not specify.

What he does tell us, however, is that Jesus knows of Peter's conversation with the tax collectors without being told about it: "What do you think, Simon? . . . From whom do the kings of the earth collect duty and taxes—from their own children or from others?" (v. 25b). Peter's answer is simple and to the point: "From others" (v. 26a). When a king levies taxes on the people, then, he doesn't include his own children in the mix. They benefit from the taxes without having to pay them.

Jesus continues: "Then the children are exempt" (v. 26b) What does he mean there?

This is a moment of self-revelation! In Luke 2:49, twelve-year-old Jesus asks the stunning question, "Didn't you know I had to be in my Father's house?" The answer here in Matthew is every bit as stunning as that moment in Luke: Jesus declares his exemption from the temple tax because he is not merely a worshiper there; he is the one worshiped. He's not a congregant; he's the only Son of the Father. Jesus uses a random encounter and a passive-aggressive question to make a bold declaration about his own identity.

What follows continues to amaze: "But so that we may not cause offense . . ." (v. 27a); we don't have to do this because I am above this, but let's pay it anyway so as not to cause people around us to stumble. It's the same concept that Paul elaborates regarding meat sacrificed to idols in Romans 14 and 1 Corinthians 8. God is not impressed with the strength of your opinion but with the depth of your sacrifice. Jesus will pay the tax to keep the peace.

He then instructs Peter to go fishing, his previous occupation before this new one of "fishing for men." He says, "Take the first fish you catch; open its mouth and you will find a four-drachma coin. Take it and give it to them for my tax and yours" (v. 27b)

Did Peter follow directions and do as he was told? Matthew doesn't say. We want to believe so, we likely should assume so, but we can't shake the memories of Peter's defiance in chapter 16—remember "Get behind me, Satan!" (v. 23)?—as well as his forthcoming denial on the eve of the crucifixion.

Perhaps by leaving the action up in the air and off the stage, Matthew is asking his readers: Will you obey even the strangest of commands? I've told you this story that looks to be about temple tax but is really about the temple's Lord. Will you obey him?

Reflect now on an area of your life that you still withhold from Jesus. You know exactly where and what it is. Today, now, surrender that to his authority and his love.

Day Fifty-Four
Matthew 18:1-9

....

When we left Jesus yesterday, he had just declared his immunity from the temple tax because he is no mere worshiper; he is the one worshiped. His analogy in explaining and revealing himself had to do with "the kings of the earth" (17:25). The implication is that Jesus is not merely one of the "kings of the earth"; he is instead the King of kings.

Picking up on that motif, the disciples open today's reading with this question: "Who, then, is the greatest in the kingdom of heaven?" (18:1).

Two things to note from this question:

1. By asking it, Jesus' disciples show they have no idea what the kingdom is really about!

2. In Mark's version of the story, the circumstances are both more detailed and more revealing. Look at Mark 9:33–34:

> They came to Capernaum. When he was in the house, he asked them, "What were you arguing about on the road?" But they kept quiet because on the way they had argued about who was the greatest.

We're not sure why Matthew omits that particular scene from his telling of the story. Does he wish to protect the reputations of Peter, James, and John? Possibly. Did he not hear this particular encounter? Doubtful. We're really left to wonder. In that process, we're grateful for Peter's self-deprecation, as he is Mark's primary source, and the stories about the disciples usually highlight his own failures.

When the question comes about in Matthew 18, Jesus answers it in much the same way as he does in Mark 9. Placing a child in their midst, he declares, "Truly I tell you, unless you change and become like little children, you will never enter the kingdom of heaven" (18:3). "Unless you change," Jesus says. What is his purpose in that? Well, this: it's his pointed way of saying, "Stop asking such ridiculous questions! Stop jockeying for position; stop climbing over one another like crabs in a simmering Crock-Pot; stop arguing over who is greater than whom! Change!"

What does he mean by "become like little children"? Not child*ish* but child*like*. There's a huge difference. Child*ish*, of course, implies self-centered foot stompers who insist on their own way. Child*like* suggests full of wonder, curiosity, and utter, complete dependence. Jesus longs to grow disciples who throw off the former in pursuit of the latter. Along those lines, remember that the communication you start with God each day is designed to lead to conversation all day long, like a child leaning on a parent.

In verse 4, Jesus doubles down: "Therefore, whoever takes the lowly position of this child is the greatest in the kingdom of heaven." We again see the upside-down nature of the kingdom of God: the first will be last, living comes through dying, greatness comes through serving, gaining through losing, and maturity through childlike dependence. It's all counterintuitive and countercultural and why those who follow Jesus will always be oddballs in the eyes of the world.

In verses 6–9, Jesus raises the stakes on how we should treat children. In this case, he means both children in terms of age and *children* who are new believers in the faith. Those who cause them to "stumble," and I assume he refers to abusers of children and false teachers of the gospel, will pay the ultimate price. When Jesus speaks of the millstone and those "to be drowned in the depths of the sea," you need to remember how terrified ancient people were of the open oceans. The sea represented chaos and turmoil. In the eyes of many, it was a malignant force whipped into a frenzy as an angry god. Many of us who have read or heard these words before fail to appreciate the terror they would have struck in the ancient mind. Jesus meek and mild this is not; this is Jesus who tells truth so that others won't have to pay the ultimate price.

The terms "eternal fire" (v. 8) and "fire of hell" (v. 9) involve the ancient term *gehenna* of fire. Gehenna was a garbage dump outside the city gates of Jerusalem that had doubled in earlier days as a place where disobedient Jews sacrificed their children to the pagan god Molech. Certain Jews in antiquity were no better than pagans, abusing and murdering their own children to please a god who does not exist.

Jesus says, "That place? That place of shame and horror and pointless exercise in pleasing a nonexistent god? That's what the afterlife is like for those who reject me and take others along with them."

Hell is that realm where too late comes too early. Those of us in Christian leadership do no one any favors when we try to eliminate its possibility or soften its terrors. It's real, it's awful, and it's forever; we know all this from the mouth of Jesus more than anyone else.

Have you said yes to the Savior who wants to rescue you from both the hell that you're headed to and the one you're going through? Today would be a good day to do just that.

Jesus saves you from both the hell that you're headed to and the one you're going through.

Day Fifty-Five
Matthew 18:10-14

H ere's a confession: I have been reading the Bible for more than
forty years. That means I have probably read Matthew twenty-
five or thirty times. And if you had asked me before I began studying
for this book, "Where is that parable of the lost sheep?" I would have
answered confidently, "Luke 15."

You'd press: "Anywhere else?"

Me: "No."

You: "Are you sure?"

Me: "Very."

You: "Positive?"

Me: "Do I have to show you my seminary degree or what? I
know what I'm talking about! It's Luke 15, part of that perfect chapter of lost things getting found, and nowhere else. Let's allow Luke to
have his moment of glory."

You: "Turn in your Bibles to Matthew 18, please."

Me: "Doh!"

Matthew 18 contains an abbreviated version of the parable of
the lost sheep. Luke 15 is a remarkable chapter, with three ascending
parables of lost things being pursued and then found: lost sheep, lost
coin, lost son(s). I encourage you to check it out for the masterpiece
that it is.

Look quickly at the different settings of this particular vignette
about lost sheep.

In Matthew 18, it's the continuation of Jesus' conversation about
humility, children, and stumbling blocks. In Luke, it is his answer to
the grumbling of the scribes and the Pharisees who are disturbed that
he spends time with tax collectors and sinners.

In Matthew, Jesus begins with a question: "What do you think?" (v. 12).

In Luke, he begins with a hypothetical: "Suppose one of you has a hundred sheep" (15:4).

In both, the disappearance of the one sheep leads to an impassioned search; though it is entirely possible that many shepherds hearing this tale would think to themselves, "Actually, I wouldn't leave the ninety-nine unprotected. I'd cut my losses with the one and protect my major investment."

In both, the shepherd has great joy in finding his lost sheep.

In Matthew, that joy is solitary. It's merely "he is happier about that one sheep than about the ninety-nine that did not wander off" (Matt. 18:13).

In both, the brief tale concludes with a reminder that the rejoicing on earth is a mirror of the joy in heaven when a lost person gets found.

What do we make of Matthew's effort at Luke's signature story? Taken both collectively and individually, what does the vignette of wandering sheep / lost sheep tell us?

God was working on you before you were looking for him. You have been the target of a relentless search by a loving God who really does not desire that any of those made in the divine image will be lost. Left to your own devices, you wander off into dangerous territory and self-destructive tendencies. But thank God, we're not left to our own devices. Instead, we're chased, caught, and kept.

If the Lord has to tell us the story twice to make sure we get it, that's just what will happen.

*God is the Great Pursuer,
and you are greatly pursued.*

Day Fifty-Six
Matthew 18:15-35

Today's reading has two very different sections. First, what appears to be almost an instruction manual for the early church, and second, a parable with a chilling knockout punch at the end. Both are closely related. Taken as a whole, they demonstrate persuasively that our vertical connection to God cannot be separated from our horizontal connection with people.

Handling Conflict in the Church

In terms of how to lead people who follow Jesus, Matthew 18 separates the amateurs from the professionals. Or, more accurately, the biblical novices from the biblically informed. Look at the beautiful process for resolving a dispute between two people in the gathering of Jesus' people:

1. Directly address the person (18:15), assertively, not aggressively. This first step in the Bible is usually the last step in practice. Why? Because so many of us are conflict avoiders! And we've never really learned to be assertive without being aggressive. Sounds like something some church should teach on sometime.

2. If there is no resolution, bring one or two others to reengage. This means respected people within church leadership to help prevent conflict avoidance and ensure peacemaking (which is much different from peace loving).

3. If there is no resolution, then, and depending on the severity of the issue, it becomes a larger matter ("tell it to the church," v. 17a). The result is to "treat him as you would a pagan or a tax collector" (v. 17b), which in one school of

thought leads to expulsion. In the other school of thought, Jesus had radical love for pagans and tax collectors! It was the respectable, religious people he struggled with! On extremely rare occasions in ministry, I have been involved in dispensing some church discipline along the lines of the first interpretation. It involved safety for congregants, and though those decisions were painful, I am convinced of their necessity. Given the choice between being a "Matthew 18 Church" and a "Sweep It Under the Rug Church," I'll take the biblical path every time.

The Parable of the Unmerciful Servant

Jesus' teaching on relationships, reconciliation, and discipline leads organically into his next parable. I love Peter's question in verse 21: "Lord, how many times shall I forgive my brother or sister who sins against me? Up to seven times?" Peter wonders, what is the most he has to do, which is another way of asking what is the least he can get away with. It's the kind of question most of us ask ourselves, at least internally, all the time.

This is the kind of question Jesus routinely sends into orbit. Here: "I tell you, not seven times, but seventy-seven times" (v. 22, also translated as "seventy times seven"). It's Jesus' way of saying, "You shouldn't even be asking that question, Peter. After all, it won't be too much longer until I'm going to have to forgive you of some very serious stuff."

Jesus follows with a parable that I suspect was ripped from the headlines, as they say on *Law & Order*. A king/master "canceled the debt" of a man who was on the verge of losing everything (v. 27). That same servant then immediately encounters one who owes him a hundred denarii, a significant sum! When his debtor begs the same kind of patience that this man has just received, he refuses: "Instead, he went off and had the man thrown into prison until he could pay the debt" (v. 30). Rules for thee but not for me.

Well, concerned onlookers go and tell the king what they have just seen, ironically, in violation of verse 15. He responds first with logic: "Shouldn't you have had mercy on your fellow servant just as I had on you?" (v. 33).

Answer: yes.

He next responds with fury: "In anger his master handed him over to the jailers to be tortured, until he should pay back all he owed" (v. 34).

Jesus then serves the knockout punch: "This is how my heavenly Father will treat each of you unless you forgive your brother or sister from your heart" (v. 35).

None of us will be in heaven because we're good enough, not even because we're better than others. We have a debt of sin we could never pay back. The glorious hymn doesn't say "Jesus Paid It Some," It reads, "Jesus Paid It All." And thus the command to us to forgive as we have been forgiven.

> ***Forgiveness happens when you say,***
> ***"This hurts but it's not the end."***

Day Fifty-Seven
Matthew 19:1-15

B efore we rush into the topic of today's reading (marriage, divorce, children), note the geography: "[Jesus] left Galilee and went into the region of Judea to the other side of the Jordan" (19:1). He is headed toward Jerusalem. Time is slowing down, and Jesus is heading toward the cross. He is perfectly executing his own execution.

What topic could get Jesus in more trouble with authorities than marriage? Look at how Matthew sets the stage in verses 2–3: "Large crowds followed him, and he healed them there. Some Pharisees came to him to test him. They asked, 'Is it lawful for a man to divorce his wife for any and every reason?'"

What should we make of the Pharisees' question? Remember: some people ask questions, not because they want an answer, but because they want an advantage. Matthew makes the Pharisees' motives clear: they "tested him," which is the opposite of "they wanted to learn from him." The question itself comes from the historic reality that in that particular time, a man could write his wife a "certificate of divorce" for almost any reason. None of today's legal protections existed, and women were treated as property. The Pharisees are asking in so many words, "What can we get away with? What's the least we can do and still stay good with God?"

Jesus' answer is not what they expect, in that he doesn't really address their question. After remarking that Moses' ancient allowance reflects not the goodness of God's design but the hardness of the human heart, he goes back to the beginning. He grounds the beauty of marriage in the reality of gender: "At the beginning the Creator 'made them male and female'" (v. 4).

Jesus goes on by going back in verse 5, which is a retweet of Genesis 2:24. Marriage is about leaving, cleaving, and becoming one. Speaking of devastating consequences, we contemporary people, as you know, generally reverse that order, putting the "becoming one" well before the leaving or the cleaving or the marrying. Again, the consequences of reversing the order can be devastating, as many of you have experienced firsthand. God really does know what's best better than we do, and sexual intimacy was God's design long before it was our desire.

I love the fact that when Jesus had a chance to redefine marriage, he reinforced it instead. When he could have made it more casual, he made it more sacred. When he could have made it convenient, he made it holy. When he could have made it about us, he reminded us it's about God. He goes back to the beginning (twice) and, in answering the Pharisees' trap, reminds his congregants of the place marriage has in God's heart from the very beginning of the human race. It is rooted in gender and reflecting God's goodness.

The next section (verses 7–9) is the subject of much conversation. Mark's version does not include the phrase "except for sexual immorality" that we find here in Matthew 19:9. Christians in the midst of divorce understandably cling to Matthew's more expansive version, especially when they have been the painful victim of a sexually immoral spouse.

The larger point is that the Pharisees minimize marriage by asking, "What's the least we can do?" Jesus elevates it by grounding it in God's design. Why would you want an easy way out when you realize the glory of God's plan? Jesus' answer shows us the many ways we ask the wrong questions. For those of you who were raised in a family where divorce happened or you have been through one yourself, you know the pain it causes as well as the goodness of God's forgiveness. No human brokenness is ever beyond the cleansing power of Jesus' blood, including the brokenness of a broken marriage and the built-in challenges of blending a family.

Look what happens in verse 10: "The disciples said to him, 'If this is the situation between a husband and wife, it is better not to marry.'" Jesus' inner circle (the disciples) have heard Jesus' answer to the Pharisees and come to him for clarification. "Given what you just said, Jesus, it sounds like we shouldn't get married at all! Please explain!" Jesus does. The answer has two parts. He begins with these words in verse 11: "Not everyone can accept this word, but only those to whom it has been given." What does that mean? The only way to live the Christian ethic is to be a Christian! Sometimes you'll hear people say things like, "I like Jesus' teaching and try to live by it, but I don't want to be a Christian or attend church." Jesus explains how that is impossible. Your holiness doesn't come via performance for Jesus but by your position in him.

I wonder if Matthew (like Mark) follows the "marriage talk" of verses 1–12 with Jesus' encounter with children (vv. 13–15) to highlight a connection between marital health and childhood well-being. Some of you know this from the experience of an intact family, and others through resilience in one that was not. Jesus blesses children as a way of reminding us of our own posture before the Father. We are powerless without God, but because of God, we are never helpless.

*It's not about your performance for Jesus
but your position in him.*

Day Fifty-Eight
Matthew 19:16-30

···

This is one of the more unsettling encounters of Jesus' ministry. It begins with a man coming up to Jesus and asking a breathless question: "Teacher, what good thing must I do to get eternal life?" (19:16). For a good number of us reading this in the 2020s, those of us who are products of the Protestant Reformation and have been schooled in "salvation by grace," we'd answer, "It's not what you do; it's what Jesus did!" And we wouldn't be wrong. But that's not where Jesus goes with his answer.

Instead, after a troublesome aside in which he seems to chide the man for asking him about "good"—though he is more likely asserting his own divinity—Jesus gives an answer that the Pharisees would likely agree with, in verse 17, an answer revolving around obedience to God's commandments.

In reading this story, most of us focus on that first question from verse 16. However, the heart of the story is in the man's follow-up questions, including verse 18: "Which ones?" Now, I don't believe he asks to gain attention; I think he wants an answer. However, his first follow-up lets us know that he wants to keep probing to find the minimum he needs to *do*; he wants to find the lowest common standard for salvation. Either that, or he wants an answer he can't abide.

Jesus answers this way in verses 18–19: "'You shall not murder, you shall not commit adultery, you shall not steal, you shall not give false testimony, honor your father and mother,' and 'love your neighbor as yourself.'" The last one is interesting, as it is not part of the Ten Commandments, and yet Jesus includes it as if it is.

Then the man asks a second follow-up, which is intriguing, because he didn't really need to. He could simply have left it alone after Jesus' first and second answers. I would likely have responded to verse 19 with: "Check, check, check, check. . . . I will see you in glory, Jesus!"

But not this guy. His second follow-up question comes at the tail end of verse 20: "What do I still lack?"

I don't know what was in his mind or heart. But something about this second and unnecessary follow-up suggests to me that he is fishing for disappointment. In some sense, he wants to be presented with an impossible task. Otherwise, why would he keep probing? Why does he continue to put the emphasis on his performance? "What else, Jesus? What more, Jesus? There has to be something else I can do and someone else I can be!"

Ultimately, Jesus complies. He gives the man what he *wants* in verse 21: "If you want to be perfect, go, sell your possessions and give to the poor, and you will have treasure in heaven. Then come, follow me."

"If you want to be perfect." The man didn't ask, "How do I become perfect?" He asked, "How do I get eternal life?" Jesus answers the question he hasn't asked because he knows something true about the man's motivation, his character, and his affections.

The man's response is unsurprising: "When the young man heard this, he went away sad, because he had great wealth" (v. 22).

The disciples watch this exchange, and Matthew tells us that they were "greatly astonished" (v. 25). Jesus had issued the enduring statement that "it is easier for a camel to go through the eye of a needle than for someone who is rich to enter the kingdom of God" (v. 24). The disciples' response is predictable: "Who then can be saved?" (v. 25).

Notice what happens next: "Jesus looked at them" (v. 26). Ah! When Jesus looks, he loves. He doesn't necessarily approve, but he does love. And he doesn't tell us what we want but does tell us what we need. In this moment with the disciples, after looking at them,

Jesus liberates them with eternal truth: "With man this is impossible, but with God all things are possible" (v. 26).

Peter can't let that one pass: "We have left everything to follow you! What then will there be for us?" (v. 27). I sense that answer must have frustrated Jesus, for it smacks of self-righteousness. In a sense, his answer parallels what the young man had declared earlier: "I've done it all!" The frustration and subtle correction emerges in Jesus' answer of verses 28–30. In those words, Jesus does, in fact, promise Peter and the others "a hundred times as much" in the life to come (v. 29), but he adds one more cautious note: "But many who are first will be last, and many who are last will be first" (v. 30). This "first last, last first" is another of his "upside-down" sayings, one that reminds these disciples—who were the first to follow Jesus—that his kingdom will upend all our notions of privilege, position, and prestige. It's also an uncanny introduction to the next parable Jesus tells . . . but we'll have to wait until our next reading to see what that is and find that out.

> **The best thing about your life is that you are utterly, completely dependent upon Jesus for all of it. Celebrate how strange that makes you in our self-sufficient world.**

Day Fifty-Nine
Matthew 20:1-16

....

Before you look at today's reading, check the verse that concluded yesterday's: "But many who are first will be last, and many
who are last will be first" (19:30). If you skip down to today's final
verse, you'll see it's the same thing: "So the last will be first, and the
first will be last" (20:16). That means we have an *inclusio*, which is a
fancy name for a bookend, a literary structure that tells us everything
in between must reinforce that which appears on either side.

What's "in between"? A parable that strikes us as strange, odd,
and most definitely unfair. We know it's a parable because of the
opening: "For the kingdom of heaven is like . . ." With that introduction, we know Jesus is preparing to give us yet another autobiography of God. "Here's what it's like to be me," is the implication.

The parable involves a landowner who begins a day at about
6:00 a.m. by hiring day laborers for his vineyard (vv. 1–2). This part
of the story made perfect sense to Jesus' original audience and Matthew's first readers, as that's how commerce and employment worked
in ancient Israel. Notice the arrangement: "He agreed to pay them
a denarius for the day and sent them into his vineyard" (v. 2). A denarius was a typical day's wages in ancient times.

At 9:00 a.m., the landowner returns to the part of the village
where workers wait and hires more. Note the arrangement for this
crew who, by definition, will work three hours less than the early
birds: "I will pay you whatever is right" (v. 4).

The same thing happens at noon, at 3:00 p.m., and finally, at
5:00 p.m. He asks of that final contingent: "Why have you been
standing here all day long doing nothing?" (v. 6) The answer: "Be-

cause no one has hired us" (v. 7). He hires them to work the last hour of the day and leaves their compensation up in the air.

At the end of the day, presumably 6:00 p.m., the landowner sends his foreman to pay the workers. The foreman is to pay the final group, those who had worked only one hour, first and then pay the others in reverse order. The late arrivers receive a denarius (v. 9), leading the rest of the crew to think to themselves, "This is our lucky day! If those guys got a denarius, imagine what we'll get for working so much more!" Natural, expected, and above all, fair.

Yet their hopefulness is misplaced, as verse 10 tells us: "But each one of them also received a denarius." Naturally, they complain. Who wouldn't? I love the heart of the complaint: "You have made them equal to us" (v. 12). They might as well have said, "What kind of karma is this? We're getting less than we deserve simply because they are getting better than they deserve!"

It's interesting that the answer comes, not from the foreman who paid them, but from the landowner who is in charge of the entire operation. His reply turns the grumbling on its head and asks three penetrating questions:

"Didn't you agree to work for a denarius?" (v. 13). Answer: yes.

"Don't I have the right to do what I want with my own money?" (v. 15a). Answer: yes.

"[A]re you envious because I am generous?" (v. 15b). Answer: Yes.

What should we make of this story in which the landowner gets to define both fairness and generosity? To answer that, we need to remember Matthew's overall intent: Jesus is the fulfillment of everything that is Israel. God sends him first to the lost sheep of Israel. Paul reminds us throughout the book of Romans that the gospel is good news "first for the Jew, then for the Gentile" (see, e.g., Rom. 2:9). On one level, the parable speaks to the ways that, although the Jews were "first" (presumably the early birds, less "hired" than "chosen" via Abraham), the Gentiles have been grafted into the kingdom. All will receive the same eternal blessing when Jesus returns. God, in divine grace, has indeed made the Gentiles "equal" to Israel.

On another level, the story proves conclusively that God is not fair. If God was *fair*, karma would be real, not just for other people but for ourselves. Yet grace overwhelms karma, and God gives us better than we deserve. If you're like me, you realize all the ways your level of blessing is greater than your level of obedience. This parable simply reveals to us how that's true on a cosmic scale.

If you've walked with Jesus faithfully for years, can you live with that? Can you embrace the truth that the guy down the street who wasted years of his life on irresponsible living can receive the same reward by faith as you? On the flip side, if you are the guy down the street who has lived a wasted-time kind of life, do you realize how God offers salvation to you until your very last moment?

God decides what's fair. God operates by grace. Whether we're first. Or last.

If God was fair, you'd get what you deserve. None of us want that. Thanks be to God for incomparable unfairness!

Day Sixty

Matthew 20:17-34

A s we begin to read today, please recall yesterday's parable of "the workers in the vineyard" (Matt. 19:30–20:16) and its book-ended refrain: "The last will be first, and the first will be last." It's an obvious challenge to all our notions of position, privilege, and power.

The disciples must not have been listening. Or, if they did hear it, they didn't like it.

The order in which Matthew arranges his material hammers home that point in a way that I imagine made his first readers and hearers laugh out loud. It starts in today's section with this narration in 20:17: "Now Jesus was going up to Jerusalem." "Up" in this case does not mean north (*up* on a map), but *up* in elevation, as Jerusalem is located on one of the highest places in all of Israel. Jesus is ascending to his execution.

Jesus tells his disciples as much in verses 18–19. He could not be more clear or more accurate in describing and then predicting his death and his triumph.

We then move on to verse 20: "Then the mother of Zebedee's sons came to Jesus with her sons and, kneeling down, asked a favor of him. 'What is it you want?' he asked. She said, 'Grant that one of these two sons of mine may sit at your right and the other at your left in your kingdom.'"

Wow.

These are fully grown adults, men who have made their way in life, and they have Mommy do their dirty work for them. They're seeking to be prime minister and secretary of defense in the coming kingdom, and yet they don't have the courage to ask it for themselves! In my mind, that's grounds for automatic disqualification.

Jesus, however, offers an answer that both rebukes and restores in verse 22:

"You don't know what you are asking . . . Can you drink the cup I am going to drink?" Still clueless, they answer, "We can," and I'd love to know if it was just the boys with that confidence or if Mom added her voice to the chorus!

Later in the Gospel, in 27:38, Matthew makes it clear just how much James, John, and Mom did not know what they were asking:

Two rebels were crucified with him, *one on his right and one on his left.* (emphasis added)

Whoa. That's the coming kingdom in which the first will truly be last, the last first, the greatest will serve, and the one who loses his life will save it. Everything "upside down" about the kingdom begins and ends with the cross. Matthew is brilliant, and Jesus is beautiful.

In Matthew 20:24–28, the other ten disciples hear of the request made by Mom on behalf of James and John. They are understandably indignant, but not for the right reason. We'd hope that their dismay is rooted in the way James and John have been so ignorant of Jesus' teaching. Instead, it seems more likely that they want the same kind of position and power as Zebedee's sons and resent that those two had asked for it first.

That's why Jesus has to circle the troops and let them know that his is a very different kind of army:

"Whoever wants to be great among you must be your servant, and whoever wants to be first must be your slave—just as the Son of Man did not come to be served but to serve, and to give his life as a ransom for many." (vv. 27–28)

Jesus will keep emphasizing the paradox at the heart of his mission until his followers get it; not all of them will.

The section closes with two blind men receiving their sight in verses 29–34. Note their insistence and their desperation: "Lord, Son of David, have mercy on us!" (vv. 30, 31). Their desperation stands in stark contrast to the disciples' ambition. As Jesus grants their request in verse 34, we realize that these two men have not just sight but insight; they know who is Lord and King in a way Jesus' inner circle still struggles to comprehend.

> **Today is a great day to choose desperation over ambition.**

Day Sixty-One
Matthew 21:1–11

....

"As they approached Jerusalem" is how this section begins. All of a sudden, things get real serious. Approaching Jerusalem is code for approaching destiny and embracing death. In the chapters to come, it will appear on the surface that events are spiraling out of control; and yet Matthew lets us know from Jesus' opening foray into the city that all of it is firmly in his hands. As I've said before, he is perfectly executing his own execution.

Today's reading, as you may well know, is the source of what we call in the church world "Palm Sunday." On the approach to Jerusalem, Jesus sends two of his disciples ahead—interesting that Matthew doesn't tell us which ones—and tells them to find a colt, untie it, and bring it to Jesus. Further, Jesus gives them the words to say to those who might ask why they are borrowing a colt that likely belongs to someone else.

Matthew 21:4 returns us to a pattern that we saw in the early chapters of the book: "This took place to fulfill what was spoken through the prophet." We then read a quotation from Zechariah 9:9. As always, Matthew wants his largely Jewish readership to know that Jesus completes and fulfills all that God had designed for Israel.

This unlikely plan works to perfection. Why? Because Jesus is orchestrating all of it! It will soon look like he is a victim of circumstance, but we know that in his sovereignty, he is victor over every situation. Jesus is in charge, not the religious leaders.

Why the entrance on a colt? Because Zechariah 9:9, written hundreds of years earlier, has already told us it would happen that way.

Rejoice greatly, Daughter Zion!

Shout, Daughter Jerusalem!

See, your king comes to you,

righteous and victorious,

lowly and riding on a donkey,

on a colt, the foal of a donkey.

Not only is Jesus making predictions that come true; he is the living embodiment of earlier prophecies made on his behalf.

Matthew ends this section on a note that's more typical of Mark: "When Jesus entered Jerusalem, the whole city was stirred and asked, 'Who is this?'" (v. 10). In Matthew's hands, the question doesn't hang in the air, unanswered. Instead, "The crowds answered, 'This is Jesus, the prophet from Nazareth in Galilee'" (v. 11).

Can anything good come from Nazareth (John 1:46)? We will find out in our next reading.

....

Jesus perfectly executed his own execution. Given that, can anything be too hard for him in your life?

....

Day Sixty-Two
Matthew 21:12–22

When we left the action yesterday, Jesus had just ridden into Jerusalem on a colt, receiving the hosannas of the crowd as his reception. Now he will begin to whittle away at his own popularity, for he has a larger purpose in mind.

Today's reading reveals his apparent grudge against a tree and his obvious disdain for commerce in the courts of God. You read both of those correctly. The connection between the two explains the way Matthew tells the story.

Matthew introduces the temple scene abruptly: "Jesus entered the temple courts and drove out all who were buying and selling there" (21:12). Not content merely to "drive them out," he also ensures that they can't engage in commerce for some time by overturning the tables of the money changers and the benches of those selling doves that pilgrims would use in sacrifices to God.

Why the aggression? Because both the money changers and the dove sellers took advantage of the poor and the displaced as they tried to honor God with their firstfruits. They caught vulnerable people in desperate situations and marked their product prices way up. Think of how much more everyday items cost in an airport store than in a regular one. This is a tumultuous, chaotic scene, one of those rare occasions in the Gospels in which what Jesus does obscures what Jesus says. In this case, what he says is the point of the whole thing: "It is written . . . 'My house will be called a house of prayer'" (v. 13).

As readers, we tend to focus on "house of prayer," but the astonishing part is the claim Jesus makes: "my house." Most of us have heard those words or read this verse often enough that we're blind to the scandal. He is claiming to be God! In a book all about Jesus' identity and authority, he reveals both in one fell swoop. The Jews built the temple—for Jesus.

With the audacity of that claim, Matthew makes sure we know that when "the chief priests and the teachers of the law saw the wonderful things he did and the children shouting in the temple courts, 'Hosanna to the Son of David,' they were indignant" (v. 15). No doubt they were. This man has claimed to be God. He has emboldened the crowds, and he must be executed. In a lot of ways, the temple scene sets in motion the chain of events that leads inevitably to the cross.

Matthew 21:18–22 then tells the story of Jesus' strange vendetta against a poor fig tree that has the nerve to be out of season for fruit bearing: "'May you never bear fruit again!' Immediately the tree withered" (v. 19). I love Matthew's comment that follows: "When the disciples saw this, they were amazed" (v. 20). I bet they were. Can you imagine the murmuring? "We knew he was eccentric, but now he's talking to trees, and the trees are listening to him! What have we gotten ourselves into?"

Nevertheless, Jesus' tree-talking and their murmuring inspires a question: How did that "tree wither so quickly?" (v. 20).

This raises a question for us: What's the connection between the cursing of a tree and the destruction of the temple practices? Answer: they both "have their season." Jesus' arrival inaugurates a new season altogether. He will dismantle the old wineskins of temple and sacrifice and replace them with the new and the evergreen of his own body as our temple and our sacrifice. You can't have resurrection unless you first have death.

Jesus uses the fig tree as an occasion to encourage his followers toward deeper and more expectant prayer. A friend of mine recently told me, "God can't wait to answer, so why would you wait to ask?"

Is there a part of your life that needs to die? A habit, custom, or obsession that is holding you back?

Day Sixty-Three
Matthew 21:23–27

D on't let this section's brevity obscure its importance, as these verses deal with two motifs Matthew highlights in his Gospel, one of them literary and the other theological. The literary device we've now learned to notice is the way that asking and answering questions propels the story of Jesus. The other recurring topic is less literary and more theological: the authority of Jesus.

Look how the section begins: "Jesus entered the temple courts" (21:23), the same courts where he'd caused such a ruckus the day before! He had to know his appearance there would not go unnoticed.

Jesus does draw a crowd, just not the friendly kind. The "chief priests and the elders of the people" accost him with two specific questions: "By what authority are you doing these things?" and "Who gave you this authority?" (v. 23). Do you remember the scene in the boat in Matthew 8:23–27? "What kind of man is this? Even the wind and the waves obey him!" In other words, just how comprehensive is this man's authority? Jesus' identity and its corresponding authority have been the thread holding this Gospel together.

Meanwhile, so has the technique surrounding the questions people ask Jesus. One of my great learnings as a pastor, which I have shared before, is that many people ask questions not because they want answers but because they want an advantage. That is certainly the case here in Matthew, and Jesus understands that. That's why he employs the same tactic against his opponents. He just does it better. He asks them, "John's baptism—where did it come from? Was it from heaven, or of human origin?" (v. 25).

Immediately, the religious authorities are in a no-win situation. They either minimize John's baptism and endanger themselves, or they acknowledge John's baptism and endanger themselves! I love the rare moment of self-awareness embedded in their answer: "We are afraid of the people" (v. 26), never a good trait in either civil or religious leadership.

Jesus has the last word, as the would-be interrogators reveal their cowardice: "We don't know"; Jesus replies, "Neither will I tell you by what authority I am doing these things" (v. 27). The religious leaders didn't really want an answer anyway; they only wanted an advantage. So why should Jesus defer to their wishes and answer their question?

Speaking of authority, I am so grateful to locate the authority of my life in a place well beyond my life. When you become your own authority, trouble ensues and disaster awaits. The best thing about your life and mine is that we are utterly, completely dependent on Jesus and his Word. I pray you celebrate how comprehensive his authority remains over our lives. You are not your own; you were bought with a price (1 Cor. 6:20). Hallelujah, you were bought with a price!

Show rigorous honesty with yourself: Do you ask questions because you want answers or because you want authority?

Day Sixty-Four
Matthew 21:28-46

W hen we left Jesus yesterday, he was sparring with the religious elite of Jerusalem while inside the temple courts, the same temple where he had overturned the money changers' and dove sellers' tables the day before.

In today's section, the sparring continues; in fact, we could say it escalates. Jesus makes his points against his opponents with two parables: "the two sons" (21:28–32) and "the tenants" (21:33–46).

The Parable of the Two Sons

This "two-son" parable is not nearly as well-known as that other one in Luke 15:11–32 (check it for comparison). It's also an indictment of the very audience Jesus is addressing.

One son is especially strange; he promises to work for his father, "but he did not go" (v. 30). Who does he represent? Who are those who "said" they would obey God and did not? The religious elite of Jerusalem. Historically, the collective history of the nation of Israel reveals a distressing cycle of sin, judgment, repentance, restoration, and more sin. Wash, rinse, repeat. (See books such as Judges, 1 and 2 Samuel, and 1 and 2 Kings.)

Who is represented by the slightly better son, the one in the story who says he won't work in the vineyard but ultimately does? The "tax collectors and the prostitutes" (see v. 32) who believed in John's baptism and, by extension, in Jesus' message. Now, I'm not encouraging you toward either of those career choices. What this text does encourage you to do is this: embrace that you really are powerless without God but never helpless because of him. Heaven is for the desperate, not for the deserving.

The Parable of the Tenants

As if what he has just said isn't offensive enough, Jesus says, "Listen to another parable" (v. 33a). I suspect the Pharisees and the scribes thought, "Do we have to? These never end well." Jesus tells this story less *to* them than *at* them.

The parable involves a man who plants a vineyard and ultimately becomes an absentee owner. Look at the details of his vineyard construction: "He put a wall around it, dug a winepress in it and built a watchtower" (v. 33b). That's Jesus' way of saying, "This is no fly-by-night operation. This is a vineyard of substance! The watchtower is being filled with quality and with protection."

The owner's next move is surprising: "Then he rented the vineyard to some farmers and moved to another place" (v. 33c) Why he does so and where he moves are not central to the story, so Jesus doesn't fill in those blanks. Because of the rental agreement, at harvesttime he sends a representative to collect "his fruit" as payment (v. 34). Is the arrangement fair? Is the owner honorable? Are the farmers able to make a good living? These questions interest us but are, again, not central to the story, so Jesus doesn't answer them.

What *is* central to the story is the escalation that follows in verses 35–36: Servant #1: seized and beaten. Servant #2: killed. Servant #3: stoned. Servants #4: treated the same way.

Remember the national history of Israel? Wash, rinse, repeat? This is particularly true of how the rich and the powerful treated prophets such as Jeremiah and Micah, prophets who gave them a message they did not want to hear.

The escalation culminates with the owner's son, including his almost naïve conviction that "they will respect my son" (v. 37). Result? "So, they took him and killed him, and threw him out of the vineyard" (v. 39). I love the detail of "out of the vineyard," as Jesus' crucifixion takes place *outside* the protective walls surrounding Jerusalem. He is cast *out* in every way.

Jesus then asks his adversaries on the "religious elite task force" to interpret the parable for him: "Therefore, when the owner of the vineyard comes, what will he do to those tenants?" (v. 40). The task force falls for it: "He will bring those wretches to a wretched end" (v. 41). In an ultimate *Gotcha!* moment, Jesus lets his adversaries know that they are the subject of the story he has just told: "The kingdom of God will be taken away from you and given to a people who will produce its fruit" (v. 43). His adversaries fall for a trap of their own making.

At last, the chief priest and the Pharisees get it in verse 45: "They knew he was talking about them." How so? How is this parable against them?

The simplest explanation—usually the wisest—is that the vineyard owner in some sense represents God; the vineyard is the promised land of Israel; the renters are God's chosen people, the Jews; and the collection agents are prophets such as Isaiah, Jeremiah, Ezekiel, and others. The Son, naturally, is Jesus himself, the teller of the story. The parable is about him. As I've suggested earlier in this book, parables are God's autobiography. This is what it's like to be God: to pour out love, protection, and grace and to receive rejection and violence in return. Again, I'm struck by the detail of verse 39, where the renters "threw [the Son] out of the vineyard." Where was Jesus crucified? Not in the city, but beyond its gates.

Matthew suggests that the punishment for those who reject the prophets and the Son will be swift and severe. Jesus also includes the detail that the landowner will give the vineyard to others. Matthew foreshadows Paul's understanding of what happens when the religious leaders within Judaism reject Israel's Messiah.

> Did they stumble so as to fall beyond recovery? Not at all! Rather, because of their transgression, salvation has come to the Gentiles to make Israel envious. But if their transgression means riches for the world, and their loss means riches for the Gentiles, how much

greater riches will their full inclusion bring! (Rom. 11:11–12)

That's how God massages the unbelievably good out of the un-deniably bad, how Jesus pours out sovereign grace even in the midst of severe punishment. That's a God I want to follow and a Savior I want to adore.

God specializes in massaging the undeniably good out of the unbelievably bad.

Day Sixty-Five
Matthew 22:1–14

Over the last couple of days, we have seen Jesus tell parables *at* the religious elite of Jerusalem as much as he tells them *to* his followers. Today continues and even intensifies that pattern.

Remember his location as he tells today's story, the parable of the wedding banquet. He remains in the temple courts, surrounded by his many adversaries and encouraged by his few followers. Yet even in that dangerous setting, his message is so urgent he tells it anyway. He is not at all a conflict avoider but instead a conflict redeemer.

The story begins with a comparison: "The kingdom of heaven is like a king who prepared a wedding banquet for his son" (22:2). Here is a clue. This is the autobiography of God; this is what it's like to be the Father in heaven. The next line is a bit confusing unless you know banquet customs in ancient Israel: "He sent his servants to those who had been invited to the banquet to tell them to come, but they refused to come" (v. 3). In ancient times, it was customary for a noble to send invitations out without specifying the precise time of the banquet. People knew they were invited, and they should be ready almost at a moment's notice. The second summons (more time-sensitive) comes when the food is prepared and the room is ready. That's what happens in verse 3, except with the disturbing twist "they refused to come."

The king sends a second round of servants in verse 4, this time highlighting the banquet's menu: "My oxen and fattened cattle have been butchered, and everything is ready." "Hey gang! Don't miss the event of the century! Maybe even of the millennium! Food, drinks, décor, and all that before the house band begins playing!"

The response in verse 5 is apathy. One went to his field. The other returned to his business. "The rest seized his servants, mis-

- 170 -

treated them and killed them" (v. 6). This justifiably enrages the king, who exacts a measure of vengeance in verse 7.

The parable turns in verses 8–10 as the king comes up with plan B. The servants return to the highways and byways, inviting and collecting "all the people they could find, the bad as well as the good, and the wedding hall was filled with guests" (v. 10). If the parable ended there, we could see two distinct meanings in it and applications from it:

1. It's another parable that doubles as commentary on the national history of Israel. The king is the Father in heaven, the son is Jesus himself, the wedding banquet is the inauguration of his reign, the first invited guests are the Jews of history, and the servants who issue the invitation are the prophets. Matthew 22:3, 6–9 gives us a vivid reminder of how the nation often treated the prophets.

2. The second group invited in verses 10 are the Gentiles, grafted into the kingdom and awaiting the full return of their Jewish brothers and sisters. The more personal application for many of us in the 2020s is that this story reminds us: (1) God will not be mocked (check v. 7), and (2) God will not be blocked. God's mission will continue. God's offer is bathed in grace and the invitation open to all, regardless of background or even life choices: "the bad as well as the good" (v. 10). God longs to partner with us in the relentless search for souls to save and people to invite.

That's if the parable ended at 22:10. But it doesn't. Instead, we get the disturbing story within a story in verses 11–14, where the king scrutinizes the crowd assembled at his feast, notices an attendee "who was not wearing wedding clothes," confronts him, receives no reply ("The man was speechless"), and then casts him into an outer darkness where there is weeping and gnashing of teeth. All in all, it seems preferable not to have shown up at all!

Jesus concludes the menacing story with this: "For many are invited, but few are chosen" (v. 14). You may have originally learned it as "For many are called but few are chosen."

What to make of this? The summary verse is one of those places to which our Calvinist friends point and say, "See? The Bible teaches predestination!" And so it is, even if with my Wesleyan/Methodist tribe I believe the weight of Scripture leans on the idea of free will (see, e.g., 1 Tim. 2:3–4).

Beyond that homage to predestinarian thinking, what else can we derive from this story?

It's a vivid reminder that we're not to trust our own goodness in securing our eternity but instead the goodness that belongs to Jesus. Why trust your goodness, which isn't very good, when you can trust Jesus, who is perfect? When you do that, you are "clothed in righteousness" as Revelation 19:8 implies.

Matthew 22:12—"How did you get in here without wedding clothes, friend?"—combined with Matthew 26:50 provides another intriguing possibility: When Judas betrays Jesus, look how the Savior addresses him: "Do what you came for, friend." Is that similarity by design? Is this the most subtle of references to Judas himself?

I suppose that's one of those questions we'll have to have answered "when we all get to heaven," which will happen when we're clothed not in our own righteousness but in Christ's.

**God's name will not be mocked,
and God's mission will not be blocked.**

Day Sixty-Six
Matthew 22:15-33

....

Today's reading consists of two scenes in which two separate groups of religious leaders, the Pharisees and the Sadducees, try to add to their evidence pile against Jesus. In both cases, they attempt to trap him by making him answer a thorny question about the intersection of faith and culture.

Matthew 22:15 makes the leaders' strategy clear: "Then the Pharisees went out and laid plans to trap him in his words." Notice the flattery in verse 16: "Teacher, . . . we know that you are a man of integrity. . . . You aren't swayed by others." The Pharisees' technique leaps out to me here because I am especially vulnerable to flattery. If people will just tell me what a great pastor or insightful preacher I am, they'll have me in the palms of their hands! Perhaps you're the same way and have learned the difference between flattery and encouragement only through painful experience.

Jesus doesn't fall for it. The question to which all this puffery leads, as you may know, involves taxation: Should we pay or shouldn't we pay taxes to Caesar? (v. 17). Look at the Lord's perception: "Jesus, knowing their evil intent . . ." (v. 18). Instead of answering directly, he uses a Roman coin as an object lesson. "Whose image is this? And whose inscription?" (v. 20). When the obvious answer comes, notice how Jesus turns the tables by making them answer a question. He introduces an entirely new element into the equation: "So give back to Caesar what is Caesar's, and to God what is God's" (v. 21). We normally use these words to justify paying taxes, and I suppose they have limited application in that realm. But that's not what Jesus' answer suggests. His answer deals with what so much of the rest of Matthew deals with: Who has authority? Who claims authority? In reminding them to give God what belongs to God—all of it—Jesus speaks for the Father. This explains why his adversaries are "amazed" at him (v. 22). Matthew reminds us that, just as the transfiguration filled his followers with awe, so does his teaching fill his opponents with wonder. They cannot outwit him, for any wit they have was given to them by him!

Scene two (vv. 23–33) involves what's known as the Levirate law, a centerpiece of the book of Ruth. Ancient Hebrew culture mimicked the practice of many of its neighbors in caring for a childless widow in a way that kept her late husband's name alive for generations. She would marry his brother. There was no safety net, no bureaucratic culture, only the security of a *bayith*—a father's house—which served as a compound for his entire extended clan.

The Sadducees, a religious subset in Judaism who competed with the Pharisees for power and influence and who did not believe in a postmortem resurrection, ask a deeply involved question. They spell out a most improbable scenario in verses 23–28, involving seven dead husbands, none of whom have any children, leading to a logical question: "Whose wife will she be" in the afterlife? You have to love their nerve, asking whose wife she will be in the afterlife that none of them actually believe in.

Jesus' answer comes as a rebuke to any of us who say, "Heaven gained another angel" whenever someone we know passes away. No. Resurrected people may be "like the angels" (v. 30; Heb. 1:14 reminds us that we are actually higher than angels), but we don't become angels. Nor do we remain as husband and wife. Jesus doesn't tell us *why* that is the case, though I strongly suspect it's because his glory is the center of that realm, not our love lives. He will be the focus of our attention more than our worldly attachments.

At this point, Jesus' answer goes a bit further: he rebukes the Sadducees' denial of the resurrection. "But about the resurrection of the dead" (v. 31), and the Sadducees' mouths dropped open in horror. "We weren't talking about that!" they must have thought. Yet

Jesus is declaring without apology and without reservation, "I got your attention to show you why your entire premise is wrong, and I'll use Moses to prove it!" God "is not the God of the dead but of the living" (v. 32). Yes, when God introduces himself as the God of "Abraham, the God of Isaac, and the God of Jacob" (v. 32)—three men who are dead when he utters these words in Exodus 3—God is making a startling claim. These three patriarchs are actually alive, just in a different realm and a different form. Why?

Because, as I have heard before, "everyone lives forever somewhere." That's right. Everyone lives forever somewhere.

Who in your circle of influence needs to hear the news that "everyone lives forever somewhere" today?

Day Sixty-Seven
Matthew 22:34-46

In our last reading, we saw Jesus in the vicinity of the Jerusalem temple, fielding questions from the religious elite. Those questions regarding marriage and taxation were asked not in innocence but in aggression, in pursuit of an advantage. As I consider previous passages from Matthew 22:1–33 and then today's from 22:34–45, I realize this is really the "trial before the trial" for Jesus. He will have his time before Pilate in Matthew 27, but this elongated question-and-answer really functions as his trial before the religious authorities.

If, in the previous scene, Jesus was on the defensive, answering questions, today he is more on offense, offering testimony.

The sole question he receives today is a test, as a man who is himself an "expert in the law" (v. 35) asks, "Of all the commandments, which is the most important?" (see v. 36). Jesus' answer must reassure friend and foe alike as he recites what our Jewish brothers and sisters call the *Shema*, Deuteronomy 6:4: "Hear O Israel, the LORD our God, the LORD is one." Whatever commandment reigns supreme must flow from that bedrock truth. In contrast to their pagan, polytheistic neighbors, the Jews' fundamental identity comes from the fact that there is but one God, and that God has chosen them to be his representatives in the world. All Jews, from the most casual to the most observant, know and recite the *Shema*.

The most important commandment becomes, "Love the Lord your God with all your heart and with all your soul and with all your mind" (v. 37; quoting Deut. 6:5). *Love* here is a decision of the will where, after surrendering to God, you begin to adore God.

Jesus then supplies a secondary answer, drawn from Leviticus 19:18: "Love your neighbor as yourself" (v. 39). Isn't it interesting that this "new wineskin," this author of a new covenant between God and humans, draws from history to define his mission? What appears new is really an amplification of what is ancient. We much less *discover* new truth than we *excavate* historic beauty. We excavate to celebrate.

Jesus next sheds new light on the connection of King David and Messiah (Matt. 22:41–46), and note the crowd's response: "No one could say a word" (v. 46). He has rendered friend and foe alike speechless. Writing one thousand years before Jesus walked on earth, David was given a hint that one of his descendants would ultimately become his Lord. Why do we believe that the Bible is inspired, eternal, and true? Because prophecy and its fulfillment are not mere *coincidences*; they are living demonstrations of a God who is firmly in control even when life looks like it will spin out of control.

This is a great day to excavate and celebrate ancient truths rather than discovering and platforming new ones.

Day Sixty-Eight
Matthew 23:1–12

Today begins a close look at one of the more challenging sections of Matthew's Gospel: the seven woes of Matthew 23. In some ways, the language here sounds unlike our more sanitized versions of Jesus. In fact, through the years, I have read some scholars who suggest that since the words sound almost *un-Jesus-y*, they are probably more Matthew's invention than Jesus' intention.

I say that we're wise to let Jesus decide what kind of Savior he will be and then follow him accordingly. He won't be boxed in to our notions of sentimentality but instead insists on being unleashed in spirit and in truth.

As we begin to look at the *woe* chapter in detail, remember the setting. Jesus is perfectly executing his own execution. He has cleansed the temple of Jerusalem, claiming it as his house; he has antagonized the religious elite by refusing to be trapped by their questions; and he has pointed out the hypocrisy rampant in the religion of Israel of the time.

All that is mere prelude to Matthew 23, when Jesus' attack on hypocrisy gains both force and precision.

Look how it starts: "Then Jesus said to the crowds and to the disciples" (v. 1). He is training his followers while educating the masses. If the targets of his ire overhear, even better.

The first subject of his attack is "the teachers of the law and the Pharisees" (v. 2). They "sit in Moses' seat," which means they have the authority to teach the received content of the first five books of the Bible, Genesis through Deuteronomy. When Jesus urges his followers to obey them in verse 3, he is affirming that the scribes and Pharisees have indeed mastered the teaching of the law, and their words are dependable.

Their actions? Not so much. "[T]hey do not practice what they preach" (v. 3), and then there's more. They add to the received word, creating laws and regulations that place unbearable loads on the lives of their congregants (v. 4).

Matthew 23:5 reveals the heart of the matter: "Everything they do is done for men to see." For any in ministry leadership, that's a sobering line. In this COVID and post-COVID world, where ministry success is often linked to *views* online, it's downright terrifying! If there is anything Jesus can't stand, it's religion for the sake of spectacle.

He gets specific with "phylacteries" and "tassels" (v. 5). A phylactery is a small box that faithful Jews (including many Orthodox Jews today) place on their foreheads and wrists. Inside the box, they place scriptures from Exodus 13 and Deuteronomy 6. I remember seeing a photograph of Bob Dylan with a forehead phylactery. I guess that was a time in his life when the answer was not so much blowin' in the wind as it was written on the scroll.

Are modern Jews guilty of the same religious ostentation as were the scribes and Pharisees? I very much doubt it. Look how Jesus goes on with his criticisms: "They love the place of honor at banquets and the most important seats in the synagogues; they love to be greeted with respect in the marketplaces and to be called 'Rabbi'" (vv. 6–7). Each one of those accusations could be levied against modern Christian preachers like me more easily than contemporary adherents of Orthodox Judaism.

Everything Jesus says in verses 2–10 is preparation for verses 11–12, words we've heard before:

> The greatest among you will be your servant. For those who exalt themselves will be humbled and those who humble themselves will be exalted.

Jesus' opening salvo in the *woe* chapter is a chilling reminder for religious leaders to avoid a faith that is primarily for display. It's an encouragement for congregants to be wary of trusting leaders who like the limelight on themselves more than the spotlight on Jesus.

....

Ask yourself: "Does my faith come from a place of devotion or a desire for display?"

....

Day Sixty-Nine
Matthew 23:13-26

This section of Matthew 23 is like sitting in the middle of a thunderclap of Jesus' wrath. It is not for those with faint hearts or sentimental faith. What is this word *woe*, and why does Jesus use it? It is a combination of righteous indignation and enduring sorrow. Jesus is, at the same time, angry with and saddened by what he sees in the religion of the scribes and Pharisees.

In the original language, the word *hypocrite* comes from the world of Greek drama and refers to an actor, or even worse, a pretender. When you peel back all the layers of Jesus' righteous indignation, that's what infuriates him the most. The religious elite are acting their faith rather than living it, preaching it without practicing it; worst of all, insisting that their followers demonstrate a level of faith and obedience that they as leaders don't even attempt.

Look at some of the specific criticisms:

The first criticism concerns "shut[ting] the door of the kingdom of heaven in people's faces" (v. 13). In other words, adding layers of man-made law to God's revealed grace, and doing so in a way designed to exclude rather than invite.

Jesus increases the seriousness of his charge with this second condemnation: turning converts into sons of hell (v. 15). What does that mean? This: when Pharisees made converts of Gentiles (turning them from polytheism to monotheism), their practice was to emphasize what it meant to be a Pharisee more than what it meant to follow God. It would be as if it were more important to me that people become Methodist than that they become Christian.

After charges against his adversaries and their attitudes toward money (vv. 16–24), Jesus summarizes his fury at the Pharisees by noting they are clean on the outside, greedy and indulgent on the inside (vv. 25–26). Jesus here circles back around to the thrust of this section, which is the difference between authentic faith and display-case faith. I have noticed that Christian faith lived primarily for public consumption almost always gets exposed for the lie that it is. I recognize this tendency in myself, as I have more than a little of the "Look at me!" or "How about what I just did!" in me. The most powerful weapon I have in my arsenal to battle this is a specific kind of prayer: I ask God to help my desires match God's design; and in those cases, obedience won't be a chore but a joy. Obedience moves from something imposed from beyond and becomes something that emerges from within.

I invite you into that same prayer journey today: ask God to help your desires for all of life to match God's design. What a thrill! You want what God wants. The result? Your searching and fearless moral inventory will lead to a clean conscience and peaceful sleep.

> *Invite God to empower you so that your deepest desires match God's grandest design.*

Day Seventy
Matthew 23:27-39

....

With this section of reading, we bring to a close the *woe* chapter. Many of you are thinking, "It's about time! This is one depressing chapter." And so it is. I suspect that the temptation is to read these words as directed at someone else and not to pause and see how they might be intended for us. Remember that as we read Scripture, we offer ourselves to let it read us as well.

The passage today begins with a repetition of what has gone before it: "Woe to you, teachers of the law and Pharisees! You hypocrites!" Again, the enemy is faith that finds its only purpose in being on display, more for public consumption than private commitment. Jesus makes that much clear in his reference to "whitewashed tombs" (v. 27), which were characteristic of ancient Israel. As you may know, coming in contact with anyone or anything *unclean* rendered ancient Jews ineligible for entrance into the Jerusalem temple. Nothing was more unclean than a dead body. To ensure that all that surrounded death was as *clean* as possible, the ancients really did whitewash stone tombs to make them gleam in the light. Jesus' audience, then, would have been familiar with both his topic and his tone. Yet he completes the thought with a gut punch: "In the same way, on the outside you appear to people as righteous but on the inside you are full of hypocrisy and wickedness" (v. 28). That which is inside is dead and decaying no matter how spruced up the exterior looks.

In verses 29–32, Jesus continues in the same vein, though this time with a historical twist: "And you say, 'If we had lived in the days of our ancestors, we would not have taken part with them in shedding the blood of the prophets'" (v. 30). That is a reference to Old Testament prophets with names you may have heard of, such as Jeremiah, Elijah, and Zechariah. Invariably, those prophets, who told kings what they needed to hear as opposed to what they wanted to hear, met with violent and bloody ends. Any attempt by the scribes and Pharisees to distinguish themselves from their murderous ancestors will prove futile, as their treatment of Jesus and his entourage will prove in both the coming days (Jesus' crucifixion) and the ensuing years (the martyrdom of the apostles in the era of the early church).

Jesus next evokes memories of John the Baptist: "You snakes! You brood of vipers!" (v. 33). Where have you hear that terminology before? From John's mouth in Matthew 3:7! Jesus then foreshadows how his own apostles will be treated: "Some of them you will kill and crucify; others you will flog in your synagogues and pursue from town to town" (v. 34). Peter, James, and John must have turned to each other and remarked with some dread in their voices: "He's talking about us." It's almost Jesus' way of placing a want ad for early church leaders. He closes the paragraph with a reference to Abel, the first victim of murder in the biblical story (Gen. 4), and Zechariah, one of the final prophets murdered in the national history of Israel, which you can read about in 2 Chronicles 24:17–25.

The final paragraph of today's reading takes on a more tender tone: "Jerusalem, Jerusalem . . . how often I have longed to gather your children together, as a hen gathers her chicks under her wings" (v. 37). This represents one of the rare occasions in which Jesus employs a feminine metaphor for God: "as a hen gathers her chicks." What a vivid reminder of what Genesis 1:27 has already told us: "So God created mankind in his own image; in the image of God he created them; male and female he created them."

That created glory gets earthy with the "like a hen" reference, which makes the letdown at the end of verse 37 that much more painful: "and you were not willing." A few other versions of the Bible render it: "but you refused."

I wonder how often that sentence is true of you and me. Jesus longs to hold us, to spend time with us, to comfort us and to challenge us, but we refuse. If that has been true in the past, today is an opportunity to make it right. Allow yourself to be held by God's power and loved in Jesus' name. He has been working on you long before you were looking for him.

> **Allow yourself to be held by God's power and loved in Jesus' name.**

Day Seventy-One
Matthew 24:1-14

A s we open up Matthew 24, the idea of what is to come dominates the atmosphere: what lies ahead in the near term, long
term, on the horizon, well beyond the horizon, and even much later
to arrive.

All those interwoven concepts characterize Jesus' teaching regarding the fate of the Jerusalem temple and, ultimately, the fate of
the earth itself in Matthew 24. If we focus too much on the first-
century applications, we miss much of what Jesus communicates. If
we focus too much on the end-time applications, we also miss much
of what Jesus communicates. It's a dilemma, but one worth our time
and effort.

Jesus' long teaching here begins with his inner circle drawing his
attention to the impressive structures that make up the temple in
Jerusalem. Jesus gives an unsettling response: "Do you see all these
things? . . . Truly I tell you, not one stone here will be left on another;
every one will be thrown down" (v. 2).

Guess what? That happened, just as Jesus foretold, in AD 70.
The Roman government, its patience taken to the limit by the ongoing rebellion of the Jews, ransacked the city and laid waste to the
temple itself. As you consider Old Testament history along with this
New Testament development, consider all those who occupied and
oppressed Israel: first Egypt, then Assyria, then Babylon, then Persia,
then Greece, and then ultimately Rome itself. Yet in our day, both
the Jews as a people and Israel as a nation stand and survive with
remarkable resilience.

So in Matthew 24:3, after Jesus predicts the destruction of the
temple thirty-seven years before it happens, the disciples ask an un-
derstandable question: "[W]hen will this happen, and what will be

the sign of your coming and of the end of the age?" Notice how their question assumes that Jesus' prophecy regarding the temple ushers in the end of all things. Jesus' answer in verses 4–8 appears to shift his focus to align with theirs. Read it carefully. Here's the summary of what to look for in anticipating Jesus' return to earth and the onset of eternity:

- false messiahs (v. 5)

- wars and rumors of wars (v. 6)

- nation rising against nation (v. 7a)

- famines and earthquakes in various places (v. 7b)

Do you see what I see? Those "signs of the end" have always taken place. From the time of Jesus until now, life on planet Earth has always included all of those elements. That lets us know that when we see those signs in front of our eyes, we're not to use them to predict but instead to prepare. Those who predict say with misplaced confidence, "Oh, this means Jesus will return in our lifetime." Those who prepare say instead, "Jesus said to 'watch' because he could come back at any time. I'm not going to try and figure out when; I'm just going to live as if it could be today." Huge difference. Predictors make charts and graphs of the end times. Those who prepare share their faith with urgency, knowing that the end will come suddenly and unexpectedly.

As Jesus continues his teaching, verse 9 apparently shifts focus back to the near term. Addressing his disciples, he lets them know their own future: "Then you will be handed over to be persecuted and put to death, and you will be hated by all nations because of me." Here Jesus gives the job description for an apostle. It is astonishing that they kept at it! Knowing it would cost them their lives, still they accepted the mission! Why? Because they saw him in his resurrected state; but I'm ahead of myself. We'll read about that in Matthew 28.

Jesus warns his followers that the persecution will destroy the love of some in the church (v. 12), "but the one who stands firm to the end will be saved" (v. 13). That last phrase is the entire book of Hebrews in a nutshell. Persecution is inevitable, so make sure your faith is unstoppable!

Matthew 24:14 shifts the focus yet again: "And this gospel of the kingdom will be preached in the whole world as a testimony to all nations, and then the end will come." The church has historically used this to emphasize our global mission imperative. Among the many reasons to saturate the people groups who have never heard of Christ with the news of Jesus is the awareness that all must have an opportunity to hear before the end comes. We know all won't say yes. Nevertheless, those of us who have said yes to Jesus did so because someone told us. We've been invited into a living relationship with Jesus Christ. Whatever else verse 14 means, it means this: the invited have the privilege of becoming the inviters.

Whom will you invite to say yes to Jesus today?

*If you encounter **end-times teaching** in which the teacher expresses certainty about when Jesus will return, run away. Do not look back; run away as fast as you can.*

Day Seventy-Two

Matthew 24:15-35

Yesterday, we began reading Matthew 24, a chapter in which Jesus answers a question his disciples ask: "When will this happen, and what will be sign of your coming and of the end of the age?" (24:3).

We saw together how Jesus' answer shifted from both the near-term future, that is, the impending destruction of Jerusalem by the Romans in AD 70, and the long-term future: his own second coming, for which we still wait!

The opening segment in today's reading refers to Daniel, who, in turn, reminds us of the Greek domination of the Holy Land in the years before Jesus. The Greeks did their best to stamp out Jewish faith, even turning the holy rooms of the priests and Levites into public brothels. At every level, the Greeks tried to eliminate Jewish thought, faith, and religion. The Greek efforts had a limited shelf life, however, as the Jews revolted under the leadership of Judas Maccabaeus. That revolution helped to reestablish Jewish life in Jerusalem by the time of Jesus. Jesus' point with the reference is that more of the same, this time at the hands of the Romans, looms in the near future.

We know from historical accounts that when the Romans destroyed Jerusalem in AD 70, in their own attempt to stamp out Jewish faith and life, it was a time of "great distress" (v. 21). Many Jews starved, others resorted to cannibalism, and still others were murdered outright by the invading army. The temple was destroyed, and Jews were scattered in what became known throughout the centuries as the *Diaspora*, the dispersal. The onslaught is how so many became part of what historians call European Jewry. The persecution never ceased, from the pogroms of Russia to the Holocaust at the hands of Nazi Germany.

As we look again at our biblical text, Jesus uses this occasion and these words to remind his people to be on guard against would-be saviors: "At that time if anyone says to you, 'Look, here is the Messiah!' or, 'There he is!' do not believe it. For false messiahs and false prophets will appear" (vv. 23–24b). In my experience, the falsest of false messiahs are those who tell us they know when these future events will occur. In my lifetime, Jesus' return was predicted with great certainty to happen in both 1987 and again in 2011. Guess what? He kept us waiting both times!

Jesus instead warns us not to let such prophets "deceive . . . even the elect" (v. 24b). Who are the *elect*? Is Jesus' talking predestination here, that he has chosen who will be saved and who will be lost? There could be a sense of that in these words, though we should be careful never to confuse *elect* with *elite*. In whatever sense the body of Christ is elect, we are elected to service, to proclamation, and often to suffering. Just ask the Jews about the *privileges* that have gone along with being God's chosen people.

....
Elect *is in fact a biblical concept. We must be careful not to confuse it with* elite.
....

Throughout Matthew 24, we've seen Jesus employ an intriguing pattern of near term / far term. He uses the pattern to speak both to the impending fall of Jerusalem in AD 70 and to his second coming at the end of days.

In today's section, we see more of this near term / far term pattern. In verses 25–28, he warns us yet again not to believe every wandering prophet or would-be messiah who claims to usher in the end: "So if anyone tells you, 'There he is, out in the wilderness,' do not go out; or 'Here he is, in the inner rooms,' do not believe it" (v. 26).

Instead, Jesus says, his return will be as sudden "as lightning that comes from the east" (v. 27), even as it follows a time of increasing global distress (v. 29a). In verse 29, Matthew links this hope with the prophetic hope of Ezekiel 32:7, and then launches into one of the most hopeful paragraphs of the entire chapter:

> "Then will appear the sign of the Son of Man in heaven. And then all the peoples of the earth will mourn when they see the Son of Man coming on the clouds of heaven, with power and great glory. And he will send his angels with a loud trumpet call, and they will gather his elect from the four winds, from one end of the heavens to the other." (vv. 30–31)

Why do I find this so hopeful? Two reasons: (1) In the midst of mourning, there is the sudden "power and glory" that will be visible to all, redeemed and unredeemed alike; and (2) even more significantly, we can tell that Paul—who never met Jesus in person—was immersed in these words. Look how Paul describes the second coming to the Thessalonian church:

> Brothers and sisters, we do not want you to be uninformed about those who sleep in death, so that you do not grieve like the rest of

mankind, who have no hope. For we believe that Jesus died and rose again, and so we believe that God will bring with Jesus those who have fallen asleep in him. According to the Lord's word, we tell you that we who are still alive, who are left until the coming of the Lord, will certainly not precede those who have fallen asleep. For the Lord himself will come down from heaven, with a loud command, with the voice of the archangel and with the trumpet call of God, and the dead in Christ will rise first. After that, we who are still alive and are left will be caught up together with them in the clouds to meet the Lord in the air. And so we will be with the Lord forever. (1 Thess. 4:13–17)

See the similarities? Jesus' coming will be sudden, there will be a trumpet call, and we will celebrate an ingathering of both "the quick and the dead" as the creeds say. There is no secret disappearance, no wondering, "What just happened?" no lingering trauma to work through for a specified amount of time.

May it be so.

Jesus' return will be sudden, spectacular, and unmistakable.

Day Seventy-Four
Matthew 24:36-51

....

What if one of the largest Christian book and film franchises hinges on a misreading of a single verse of Scripture? What if God used that franchise for good, more in spite of its biblical understanding than because of it? What if a whole lot of us need to rethink what we learned, read, and watched in the late '90s and early '00s?

What if you really want to be *Left Behind*?

Now: if you're not aware of the books, movies, T-shirts, and bumper stickers around all the Left Behind franchise, feel free to read what follows with mild interest. If you're a card-carrying Left Behinder, please read with an open mind. If you've been at a church with solid and comprehensive teaching about the end times, perhaps you'll read this in a way that makes you nod in agreement.

Here's the situation. As Jesus winds up his teaching in Matthew 24, he moves away from the soon-and-very-soon destruction of Jerusalem (AD 70) and into the end of all things. That's his focus in 24:36-51. He begins with a forceful rebuke of all predictors and a thorough comfort for all preparers:

> "But about that day or hour no one knows, not even the angels in heaven, nor the Son, but only the Father." (v. 36)

The passage pivots at verse 37: "As it was in the days of Noah, so it will be at the coming of the Son of Man." Well, what happened in the "days of Noah"? One family built an ark while the rest "were eating and drinking, marrying and giving in marriage, up to the day Noah entered the ark" (v. 38). *They*—everyone not in Noah's family—are the subjects of this section of Jesus' address. Not Noah. The non-Noahites! Notice that. It matters.

So what was the fate of all these who were the subjects of Jesus' discourse? "[T]he flood came and took them all away" (v. 39a). Oh wow. It swept them away. Noah and family (oh, and animals), meanwhile, remained in the ark: stable, secure, not swept away but left behind. Jesus presses the point home in verses 39b-41:

> "That is how it will be at the coming of the Son of Man. Two men will be in the field; one will be taken [as in, swept away!] and the other left [like Noah!]. Two women will be grinding with a hand mill; one will be taken and the other left [Ditto!]."

Be like Noah. Don't be like the rest. You want to be in the *ark* of faith when I return, Jesus is saying, so you're not swept up and away in the cauldron of judgment.

The premise of the Left Behind franchise, in case you don't know, is the opposite: seven years before the real Second Coming, there is a rapture of the church, in which Christians are taken away and the unbelievers are *left behind* for seven years of tribulation before the actual Second Coming. That's literally what happens in scene 1 of the first novel and movie. It's actually a pretty compelling scene in which a copilot disappears from a jet cabin (because he's a Christian), leaving behind his pilot friend, who now has to both land the plane and figure out how to navigate the seven years! Pretty good fiction. Not very good theology.

One verse matters. Context is everything. God is good to use even (what I believe is) a biblical misreading to bring people to faith. Some of you, in fact, may have become a Christian through the Left Behind series. If so, praise God. Now you know that God is bigger than any reading or understanding of Scripture.

Now that we've got that cleared up (unless you're really mad at me now), Jesus spends the rest of this chapter exhorting his followers to "keep watch, because you do not know on what day your Lord will come" (v. 42, in contrast to *Left Behind*, in which you know he's coming seven years after you were left behind from the rapture! I know: I'm piling on.)

What will we be found doing when he returns? Not studying the charts of what's supposed to happen next. Instead, studying the Word to see how we might live faithfully now. Treating our fellow servants well as opposed to abusively (v. 49) and waiting in humility rather than living in arrogance.

Jesus is coming back. Suddenly. Emphatically. Unmistakably. Victoriously. It could be today. It could be many generations from today. When he does, I plan to be resting in the ark of faith, and I hope you'll join me and invite others.

Spend less time predicting the date of the Second Coming and more time preparing for its inevitability.

Day Seventy-Five
Matthew 25:1–13

I have shared before that neither Matthew nor the other biblical authors wrote their books with *chapters* and *verses* in the text; church leaders and Bible scholars added those hundreds of years later. Today's reading is an example of a chapter division that is not especially helpful, as we're tempted to think chapter 25 is something new and different from chapter 24, when, in fact, it is a continuation of it. Jesus has been speaking in ominous terms about the impending destruction of Jerusalem as well as his second coming at the end of all days. Now he will tell three parables in a row that are windows into what Messiah's return will be like. Today we'll look at the least well-known of the three, a parable called "the Ten Virgins."

Notice how it begins in verse 1: "At that time the kingdom of heaven will be like . . ." The logical question for us is, "At what time, Jesus?" By keeping the importance of context ever in front of us, we surmise that "that time" refers to what Jesus has just finished talking about at the conclusion Matthew 24: his own return to judge the quick and the dead. As we saw in yesterday's reading, that return will be sudden, emphatic, and unmistakable. It will bring salvation to those who have surrendered in faith and abject terror to those who have not.

The story that Jesus develops here in the opening words of Matthew 25 is odd to our ears, but it made perfect sense to his original audience. In the villages of ancient Israel, a wedding was no one-day affair. In fact, the festivities often took place over the period of a week. The couple did not go away for a honeymoon but instead received the well-wishes of the villagers throughout the prescribed wedding period.

Further, it was common for the bridegroom to make surprise appearances, even in the middle of the night, and to send a messenger ahead of him, calling out in the streets, "Behold, the bridegroom is coming!" Finally, in the villages of ancient Israel, women were not allowed on the streets at night without a lamp. This is all a long way of saying that Jesus' story comes from the very fabric of the lives of the people to whom he tells it.

Matthew 25:2 tells us in advance what will happen in the parable: "Five of them were foolish and five were wise." The wise virgins took not only their lamps but also extra oil to keep them lit, while the foolish ones only brought the oil that was already in their lamps.

All ten fall asleep (v. 5), suggesting that Messiah's return will be delayed enough that all people, prepared or not, will at some point become distracted.

Look at verse 6: "At midnight the cry rang out: 'Here's the bridegroom! Come out to meet him!'" Sudden, unexpected, unmistakable, just as we have seen throughout Matthew 24.

Yet the sudden arrival brings about a dilemma for the foolish virgins. They have to borrow oil from the ones who had prepared in advance. The answer of the wise virgins appears a bit selfish: "No . . . there may not be enough for both us and you. Instead, go to those who sell oil and buy some for yourselves" (25:9). Through that veneer of self-centeredness, we see a deeper point. When Jesus does come, you won't be judged based on someone else's faith or lack thereof. You'll be judged on you.

Well, while the five foolish virgins go oil shopping, the bridegroom arrives, the wedding begins, "and the door was shut" (v. 10). The virgins plead that the door open so they might enter in. Instead, the reply comes back emphatically: "Truly I tell you, I don't know you" (v. 12). We've seen that same sad drama before in Matthew 7:21–23.

Jesus summarizes his own story: "Therefore keep watch, because you do not know the day or the hour" (v. 13).

What to make of this story? Two themes leap out:

1. You can't borrow someone else's faith. You may inherit it—and many do—but at some point you have to claim it as your own. When Jesus returns, he won't ask you what your friends or family did with him; he will ask, "What did *you* do with me?"

2. Since distraction is inevitable, preparation is essential. Instead of predicting when Jesus will return, be ready for him to come back today. I don't want *too late* to come *too early* for anyone reading these words.

Do you merely borrow your faith from parents or friends . . . or have you claimed it as your own?

Day Seventy-Six
Matthew 25:14-30

M atthew 25 consists of three long parables. Yesterday, we looked at the parable of the ten virgins, today it's the parable of the talents, and then we'll dig into the parable of the sheep and the goats. All three deal with the end times. All feature an authority figure who either returns or appears, and all three involve the ultimate separation of those who are saved from those who are lost. In other words, all three have immense promise and implied warning.

The parable of the talents is another example of Jesus' teaching that has both an immediate application (and even accusation) for his original audience as well as a longer-term understanding for you and me. Let's look at how it begins: "Again, it will be like a man going on a journey, who called his servants and entrusted his wealth to them" (25:14).

What follows is a dispersal of that wealth. Some translations refer to the monetary unit as a "talent" while the NIV calls it "bags of gold." Matthew wrote in Greek, and the word in question transliterates as *talanton*, a way of determining value by measuring weight. From our perspective, the specific amount is less important than the fact that the three men in question are entrusted with different measures. Most experts believe that a "talent" or a "bag of gold" represents an enormous sum of money and a remarkable degree of trust on the part of the master.

One man receives "fives bags of gold," another gets "two bags," and then the third man "one bag" (v. 15a). Notice the criteria: "each according to his ability" (v. 15b). What ability? Their ability to invest well? To start a business? To arrange an IPO? To invent a product the world didn't even know existed but once released people couldn't live without it? We don't know because Jesus doesn't say.

Matthew 25:16–18 summarizes what the three men do with their bags of gold: Five Bag Guy doubles his, Two Bag Guy does the same, and One Bag Guy "went off, dug a hole in the ground and hid his master's money" (v. 18).

The key phrase? "His master's money." Whatever gifts or abilities or even wealth we possess is actually on loan. We're responsible for how we use it, not because it is ours, but because it isn't.

In keeping with the three parables of Matthew 25, the master returns to settle accounts (v. 19). Five Bag Guy (v. 20) and Two Bag Guy (v. 22) report on their doubled investment. The overjoyed owner promises that they will "share [their] master's happiness" (vv. 21, 23). So far, so good.

But One Bag Guy offers a prelude to his strategy of burial versus investment: "I knew that you are a hard man, harvesting where you have not sown and gathering where you have not scattered seed" (v. 24). He presumes to have insight into his master's character and motivations, and, as we have seen, his assumptions are not accurate. The master responds with great fury (v. 26), and the man's first punishment is to give his one bag to Five Bag Guy (now, suddenly, Eleven Bag Guy). The rationale? "For whoever has will be given more, and they will have an abundance. Whoever does not have, even what they have will be taken from them" (v. 29). Our fearful non-investor finds himself *outside*, just like the foolish virgins in the previous story, though with the added horror of "where there will be weeping and gnashing of teeth" (v. 30).

In the immediate setting, Jesus is likely telling another story *at* his religious opponents. One Bag Guy represents the scribes and the Pharisees, those who have been entrusted with the oracles of God and have buried them, nursed them, and protected them. They have not sought to share them and expand them. When your own goal is religious preservation rather than gospel expansion, then even what you have will be taken away.

In the longer-term view, the thrust of the parable is in verse 29 and its insistence that we understand that whatever gifts we have, whether our wealth or intelligence or charm or strength, are on loan. We're accountable because we're stewards and not owners.

I am certain that many of you reading this book have abilities in ministry that have yet to be unleashed. Some of you have a call to start new churches. Others have a call to undertake mission work across the globe. Others have been in small group studies for years and you now realize while you read this that you should be leading one. Finally, I suspect that most, if not all, of you have a *one*, someone in your life with whom you now know that God is inviting you to share your faith.

> **Whether it's leadership capacity or material favor, all we have is on loan. We are stewards, not owners, and we will give account for how we handled what we borrowed.**

Day Seventy-Seven
Matthew 25:31-46

....

Today's parable, usually called "The Sheep and the Goats" brings Jesus' lengthy end-times conversation in Matthew 24–25 to a close. Do you remember what set it all up? His disciples were asking, "When will this happen, and what will be the sign of your coming and of the end of the age?" (24:3). Through it all, his answers have dwelt on our need to avoid predicting and instead embrace preparing.

As we'll see shortly, this closing parable presents a major dilemma in terms of interpretation, a dilemma that actually goes to the heart of understanding Christianity itself. But don't worry. I think we'll work it out.

Notice the role of the word *glory* as Jesus opens: "When the Son of Man comes in his glory, . . . he will sit on his glorious throne" (25:31). What a vivid reminder that the afterlife is so much less about reuniting with people we have loved and so much more about gazing in eternal joy at the One who secured our place in heaven. It's not a better version of earth in which we do all those things we did here; it is, instead, an entirely different realm that is untouched by sin and ruled by grace.

Then at verse 32, we read, "All the nations will be gathered before him, and he will separate the people one from another as a shepherd separates the sheep from the goats." Notice: the separation has already been made, based apparently on some preexisting criteria. Tuck that away.

In verse 34, we learn that the sheep will "take [their] inheritance, the kingdom prepared for you since the creation of the world." The reason for their receiving publicly what was already theirs all along? Verses 35–36 substantiate it:

- You fed the hungry.

- You gave drink to the thirsty.

- You invited the stranger.

- You clothed the naked.

- You looked after the sick.

- You visited those in prison.

That's quite a list! The list could also make up the Mission & Outreach budget of almost any local church.

The *sheep* are bewildered with this news; in verses 37–39 they ask, "When did we [do all this]?" The King answers memorably: "Truly I tell you, whatever you did for one of the least of these brothers and sisters of mine, you did for me" (v. 40). Works of mercy and charity, done without calculation for merit or reward, look to be a vital expression of salvation.

The goats? Not so much. Check verse 41: "Depart from me, you who are cursed, into the eternal fire prepared for the devil and his angels." Well, there goes the supposed conflict between the "love of Jesus" and the "wrath of hell." What's the reason for the damnation of the goats? Verses 42–44 list all the good they left undone and verse 45 provides the chilling summary: "Whatever you did not do for one of the least of these, you did not do for me." As if we missed the point, verse 46 gives the final verdict for goats and sheep: "Then they will go away to eternal punishment, but the righteous to eternal life."

Earlier, I alluded to an interpretive challenge with this parable. Here it is. At first glance, "The Sheep and the Goats" appears to teach salvation by works. Your eternity is determined by how you treat "the least" (leaving unanswered your fate if you are one of the least). Yet that concept flies in the face of the tenor of the rest of the New Testament, which teaches salvation by grace through faith. Among those verses that are unequivocal in that regard, please check Ephesians 2:8–9: "For it is by grace you have been saved, through faith—and this is not from yourselves, it is the gift of God—not by works, so that no one can boast."

Do we have a "Gospel of Paul" that is somehow different from the "Gospel of Jesus"? Not at all.

I believe the key to resolving this dilemma is in Matthew 25:32, where the separation into sheep and goats has already occurred. The verdict has already been announced. Jesus presents the works of mercy and charity (or lack thereof) as evidence for the faith of the sheep and for the lack of faith for the goats. Salvation really is by faith, just not a dead faith, as Jesus' brother will tell us in James 2:26. I suppose that's why we call it a living relationship with Jesus Christ.

How we treat those on the margins does not so much earn salvation as reveal it.

Your treatment of others
doesn't earn your salvation;
instead your treatment of others reveals it.

Day Seventy-Eight
Matthew 26:1-16

Jesus introduces the final act of his own drama with his words to his followers in 26:2: "As you know, the Passover is two days away—and the Son of Man will be handed over to be crucified." This is a general statement that the bulk of Matthew 26 and 27 will then particularize. Through it all, we'll see how Jesus perfectly executes his own execution.

In 26:3–5, we see the origins of the Jesus plot. Notice the cynicism of the religious elite. They want to arrest and kill Jesus, but not at the expense of their own reputation and safety.

We next move to a scene in verses 6–13 that appears in various forms in all four Gospels: Jesus anointed with perfume. In each case, a woman acts extravagantly, even wastefully, to demonstrate her devotion to Jesus. When John tells the story (12:1–8), he names the woman Mary, the sister of Martha, and locates the event at a dinner party that honors recently dead, now-back-alive Lazarus. It's likely the only dinner party in the history of the human race in which the guest of honor used to be dead. In Luke's account, it takes place much earlier in Jesus' ministry (Luke 7:37–38), and the anointing woman has a much more questionable backstory.

In Matthew's telling (echoing Mark 14:1–9), here are several items to note about the anointing:

- The encounter takes place "in Bethany in the home of Simon the Leper" (Matt. 26:6). This would be just on the outskirts of Jerusalem and in a home that a proper religious person would avoid. Jesus was never one to follow the current laws of propriety, especially when it came to people you'd avoid as opposed to those you embrace. The theme of welcoming in outsiders that Matthew puts in the book's open genealogy continues to shape how he propels the narrative.

– The unnamed woman pours "an alabaster jar of very expensive perfume" on Jesus' head (v. 7). In all four Gospels where this happens, the authors want us to understand that there is no way to outgive Jesus. Whether a notorious sinner, as in Luke 7, or a woman with a more acceptable social standing, as in the other three Gospels, when you realize the depth of your rescue, there is no limit to the level of your gratitude.

– The disciples' response? Tone-deaf: "When the disciples saw this, they were indignant" (v. 8). Jesus rebukes their calculating indignation in a way that displays yet again how he is executing his own execution: "When she poured this perfume on my body, she did it to prepare me for burial" (v. 12).

– Jesus' concluding promise in verse 13—"Wherever this gospel is preached throughout the world, what she has done will also be told, in memory of her"—is proving accurate this very day. We're still talking about her!

All in all, these scenes of extravagant love serve to remind us that when you think you deserve grace, your gratitude is muted. When you realize you don't, your thanksgiving overflows.

After that extravagance, Matthew moves quickly to Judas' betrayal in verses 14–16. The contrast is jarring: a vial of perfume, which in those days was almost priceless, and now a traitor's compensation, which is precise: "thirty pieces of silver" (v. 15). Jesus has already asked, "What good will it be for someone to gain the whole world, [or thirty pieces of it!] yet forfeit their soul?" (Matt. 16:26). Now we know. We'll ponder Judas' motivations later. For now, it's enough to note that Matthew highlights Judas's calculating character in vivid contrast with the woman whose story precedes his.

The immediacy and the contrast of the two scenes are Matthew's way of asking: Which are you? One who puts demands on Jesus in a way that suggests you think you deserve grace? Or are you instead keenly aware that you don't deserve (and can't escape) his love and so your gratitude knows no bounds?

When you realize the depth of your rescue, there is no limit to the level of your gratitude.

Day Seventy-Nine
Matthew 26:17-35

If you have a Bible with section headings, yours likely says "The Last Supper." It's tempting to jump right ahead to Jesus' establishment of Holy Communion. If you do that, however, you miss the much larger point. Let me show you what I mean.

Matthew 26:17 lets us know the Festival of Unleavened Bread has begun. This is a seven-day celebration of the Jews' escape from slavery in Egypt, including the miraculous Passover, when the Hebrew firstborn were spared the plague that took the Egyptians' firstborn. It involves a sacred meal, and the disciples want to do it right: "Where do you want us to make preparations for you to eat the Passover?"

Jesus answers by sending the group into the city, where they are to find a man and then, essentially, invite themselves to dinner at his home (v. 18). Ponder that plan: Follow that guy around town. Introduce yourselves. Tell him that "the Teacher" needs a guest room where he can celebrate the meal with his disciples. He'll agree to all of it. Then make preparations there.

This is a ridiculous plan! And yet it all comes to pass precisely as Jesus said it would. Matthew 26:19 says it simply: "So the disciples did as Jesus had directed them and prepared the Passover." That might just be his greatest miracle of them all!

Let's look more deeply. Things are preparing to spin out of control—Peter's denial, the sham trial, the flogging, the abandonment, and then the crucifixion. Matthew wants you to know that Jesus is in control of all of it. He is in control of what will spin out of control. He is perfectly executing his own execution.

The impending betrayal doesn't surprise Jesus (vv. 20–21). His declaration regarding Judas in verse 24, "It would be better for him if he had not been born," raises the eternal question of God's sovereignty and our free will. Which is it? The answer: both. In a way that I doubt we'll ever fully comprehend on this side of the grave, God is sovereign, and yet we are accountable for our actions. *We* in this case includes Judas. Matthew skillfully repeats the disciples' plaintive question of "Surely you don't mean me?" twice: once in their collective voice (v. 22) and once from the mouth of Judas himself (v. 25). Isn't it interesting that Jesus' answer to the collective question indicates "No, not you" while in answering Judas he would say, "You are exactly who I am talking about" (see vv. 23–25).

The Last Supper is almost an anticlimax. Notice the verbs: Jesus takes, thanks, breaks, gives. Those are always the four actions of the Eucharist: taking, thanking, breaking, giving. Jesus does the same with the cup in verse 27, absent the breaking.

Now look at verse 30: "When they had sung a hymn, they went out to the Mount of Olives." Was it "How Great Thou Art"? Not written until 1953! "Amazing Grace"? About seventeen hundred years too early for that one as well. Whatever hymn it was, be assured of this: it was part of Jesus' plan all along.

Matthew follows the Last Supper with a brief encounter between Jesus and Peter that is full of irony and woe. Jesus lets them know that in fulfillment of Zechariah 13:7, "you will all fall away" (v. 31). To no one's surprise, Peter responds first and loudest: "Even if all fall away on account of you, I never will" (v. 33). I have mentioned this before, yet it merits repeating; the New Testament is remarkable for the way it shows the flaws of its heroes. Most ancient religious books give one-dimensional characters, who do only what is right and good. In the New Testament, we see fully developed ones, foibles and all. It's one of those features that makes the Bible more trustworthy, not less so.

Jesus lets Peter know that not only will he deny his Savior; he'll do it three times (v. 34). Peter doubles down on his declaration of fidelity. The other eleven (including Judas) join in the chorus: "And all the other disciples said the same" (v. 35). This may be the greatest case of overpromising and under-delivering in the Bible. Take a sneak peek ahead at verse 56 to see how it all turned out: "Then all the disciples deserted him and fled."

> **Matthew's focus on the disciples is a reminder for us to be wary of overpromising and under-delivering.**

Day Eighty

The disciples occupy much of the center stage of this well-known scene taking place in the Garden of Gethsemane. Reading it, I am struck by the common phrases that have been lifted from it and used in contexts that have so little to do with it.

Jesus takes his inner circle to the garden: "He took Peter and the two sons of Zebedee along with him" (v. 37). When was the last time he went away with these three? Not since the transfiguration in Matthew 17! In that scene, Jesus' turns *inside out* and reveals himself in his full, radiant glory. This is almost the reverse, turning *outside in*, in a rare moment of stress and despair: "he began to be sorrowful and troubled" (v. 37).

Matthew 26:39 captures all the pain and pathos of carrying the weight of the world on his back. For those of us who draw our doctrine of Christ from places like Colossians 1:15–20, this is a startling scene. Our Cosmic King is at the same time our Suffering Servant. In his flesh, he'd prefer not to go through the torture that awaits; he'd rather put a pause in this plan of executing his own execution. The fight within is every bit as real as the ultimate resolve to continue: "Yet not as I will, but as you will." We often add that line to the end of our prayers, naively unaware of the real weight of its first utterance.

Then the drama gets thick because the focus returns to the sleepy trio of Peter, James, and John. Peter has just emphatically insisted he'll be loyal to the end. Once again, Peter overpromises and under-delivers. When Jesus "returned to his disciples [he] found them sleeping" (v. 40). Jesus' frustration then boils over into a second command to: "Watch and pray so that you will not fall into temptation. The spirit is willing, but the flesh is weak" (v. 41). This is a phrase we lift from its original setting and use with a chuckle when we fail to live up to our better natures. Yet there was nothing funny about its first utterance.

In the symmetrical way Matthew tells his story, Jesus finds the men asleep "again" (v. 43) and then the third time (v. 45). Three verbal denials are coming from Peter, despite his denial that he'll be a denier! But before that, there are three *sleepy* denials by Peter, James, and John. It's almost enough to make you think that Matthew already wants the number three in our minds as he looks ahead to chapter 28!

Before we get there, we have to deal with the betrayal that surrounds the scene. Betrayal from Peter. Betrayal from Peter, James, and John. And now the unkindest cut of all: "Rise! Let us go! Here comes my betrayer!" (v. 46).

"While he was still speaking Judas, one of the Twelve, arrived" (v. 47a). Again, most of us knew this was coming, but we have a two-thousand-year advantage on the original hearers of the story. Many of the Gospel's first readers and hearers might well have had their breath taken away. "Judas?! I wasn't expecting it to be him!"

Notice the skill with which Matthew adds one detail to the betrayal: "With him was a large crowd armed with swords and clubs" (v. 47b). What has followed Jesus all around in this Gospel, from the first chapter to right now? That's right! Crowds. He can't escape them. Usually, they are begging for a miracle, clamoring for some teaching, or even praising with palm branches. Now they come brandishing their swords and clubs. Notice that this crowd was sent from the religious elites; it was not composed of them. They sent other folks to do their dirty work.

Judas betrays Jesus with a kiss (v. 49). Then comes one of the more interesting encounters in any of the Gospels: "[O]ne of Jesus' companions reached for his sword, drew it out and struck the servant of the high priest, cutting off his ear" (v. 51). Now, in John's version

(18:3–11) we find out the identity of the swordsman: Peter. It's interesting that Matthew does not identify Peter in this case, as he usually has no trepidation about pointing out that disciple's flaws. In Luke's telling of this same tale (Luke 22:47–51), he adds the detail that Jesus heals the man's ear. None of the other Gospels mention that rather important fact. Is it because Luke is a doctor? Perhaps. One final note: Peter already had the sword, for the text says, "he drew his sword." I don't often associate any of the Twelve as having their concealed-carry permit, but apparently they were expecting trouble and knew how to use their weapons.

In any event, Jesus does not say, "Well done! Let's get 'em, boys!" Instead, he points out the irony that this same crowd has been listening to his teaching in the temple all week long. Only now, under the protection of darkness, do they dare to arrest him. And he adds this note: "How then would the Scriptures be fulfilled that say it must happen in this way?" (v. 54). Jesus is in control of every event that appears to be spinning out of control. He has a destiny, written long ago; he is living into it; and from Matthew's opening words this Gospel wants us aware of it. Even his betrayal and arrest is the perfect execution of his own execution.

Matthew 26:56 is perhaps the saddest verse in Scripture: "Then all the disciples deserted him and fled." Contrast that with the disciples' promise of verse 35, as Peter declares, "I will never disown you," then "all the other disciples said the same." I have to think that as painful as Judas' betrayal was to Jesus, the abandonment of the other eleven must have been even greater.

Fortunately, that's not the case with our Savior. He lives up to his promises. In the meantime, we get the reminder to "watch and pray," whether in the Garden or for the end of time.

Who can you tell today that God is not just the God of the second chance but of another chance?

Day Eighty-One
Matthew 26:57-68

When we last left Matthew, he recorded one of the saddest observations in the entire New Testament: "Then all the disciples deserted him and fled" (26:56).

Today, the action centers on Peter, and the exquisite level of detail lets you know that the memories of this night stayed with the apostle for the rest of his life.

Events will spin out of control today. The verbs will increase in intensity, and it will look as if Jesus is the victim of all of it. In spite of what appears on the surface, remember that Matthew goes to great lengths to remind you of Jesus' sovereignty over the entire process. He will drop a major clue into this reading to reinforce that fact.

Look at verse 57: "Those who had arrested Jesus took him to Caiaphas the high priest." The authorities *took* Jesus. Again, it appears as if he is helpless and powerless in the face of this now venomous crowd. Yet we next see Peter: "Peter followed him at a distance, right up to the courtyard of the high priest. He entered and sat down with the guards to see the outcome" (v. 58). Immediately, we see that Peter's impending cowardice is wrapped up in his comfort. Instead of standing with the Savior, he is among the watching crowd. He has moved from participant to observer. His disengagement is but a prelude to his denial.

An interesting pattern emerges in the witness testimony against Jesus: "The chief priests and the whole Sanhedrin were looking for false evidence against Jesus so that they could put him to death. But they did not find any, though many false witnesses came forward (vv. 59–60). What do you do when the facts don't back you up? You invent new ones!

"Finally two came forward and declared, 'This fellow said, "I am able to destroy the temple of God and rebuild it in three days"'" (vv. 60–61).

After that testimony (likely of the bought variety!), the high priest addresses Jesus directly. His reply? "But Jesus remained silent" (v. 63).

Matthew's audience would have immediately connected that silence with Isaiah 53:7, written hundreds of years before this night and yet an almost perfect synopsis of it: "He was oppressed and afflicted, / yet he did not open his mouth; / he was led like a lamb to the slaughter, / and as a sheep before his shearers is silent, / so he did not open his mouth."

Who is in control of these events? The Messiah, who is so in control that he relinquishes control. Nothing took him by surprise as the events unfolded in all their God-hating darkness.

The high priest tries one more time: "Tell us if you are the Messiah, the Son of God" (Matt. 26:63b).

And now it's time for the silence to end. In an answer that evokes both Psalm 110:2 and Daniel 7:13, Jesus declares:

> "You have said so . . . But I say to all of you: From now on you will see the Son of Man sitting at the right hand of the Mighty One and coming on the clouds of heaven." (v. 64)

Jesus' affirms that he is the Messiah and does so in a way that claims even more: I am the fulfillment of the messianic promises put forth in the Hebrew Scriptures. No wonder the high priest tears his clothes (v. 65)—an ancient sign of grief and distress. A man has just claimed to be God, and the religious elite responds with grief, despair, and violence.

Now, look at verse 66: "He is worthy of death."

Then the verbs escalate in verse 67: They spit; they struck; they slapped; they taunted.

Matthew deploys his most vivid verbs to capture the brutality of this moment. The pain must have been excruciating and the humiliation enduring. However, I doubt any of the blows or any of the insults caused as much hurt to Jesus as what happens in the next scene.

Jesus is not only the agent of creation; he is the glue that holds it together. That means he's the glue holding you together, today.

Day Eighty-Two
Matthew 26:69-75

Consider what we know of Peter to this point.

- He is the one of the first to say yes to Jesus' call to discipleship.

- His mother-in-law receives one of the first healing miracles.

- He is the first human to identify and then declare, "You are the Messiah" to Jesus.

- He is also the first human to lecture Jesus on what kind of Messiah he needs to be, and that doesn't end well at all.

- He is one of the three to witness the transfiguration.

- He has emphatically promised, "I will never disown you!"

- He has cut off the ear of the high priest's servant.

- He has been at the center of the action in this Gospel and at the time of the Gospel's writing and distribution, he was a much recognized and respected authority.

With all that, Matthew is not at all hesitant to chronicle Peter's greatest failure. It's a stunning piece of writing and a remarkable lesson in church leadership. It makes me all the more grateful that in its inspiration, Scripture is full of the feats and foibles of its leading characters.

We've already seen that Peter prefers to sit with his enemies rather than stand with his Savior (v. 58). In today's reading, he is below "in the courtyard" while Jesus is "above" and on trial. There "a servant girl" approaches him. When she sees Peter she says simply, "You also were with Jesus of Galilee" (v. 69). How did she know? Had she seen him? More to the point, did she see through him?

Notice the matter-of-fact and public nature of denial #1: "I don't know what you're talking about" (v. 70). Check out the unnecessary escalation of lies. Not only does he not know Jesus; he doesn't even know what or who they're talking about.

Matthew then tells us that "another servant girl saw him and said to the people there, 'This fellow was with Jesus of Nazareth'" (v. 71). Notice again how she "saw" him. Her perception contrasts with Peter's deception. The Holy Spirit is using Matthew's artistry and skill to create a memorable yet morbid scene.

Denial #2 is more emphatic: "He denied it again, with an oath: 'I don't know the man!'" (v. 72). What do you do when you're caught in a lie? Lie harder, of course!

Finally, the burden of accusation shifts from the servant girl to the crowd itself. Peter's accent has betrayed him in the same way he is betraying Jesus. Imagine someone with a deep Southern accent on the streets of Brooklyn. It wouldn't take long for the natives to notice and conclude that a visitor from some distance away was among them. The crowd confronts him with: "Surely you are one of them; your accent gives you away" (v. 73).

Now Peter loses the temper for which he is somewhat famous. Denial #3 escalates in vehemence and absurdity: "He began to call down curses and he swore to them, 'I don't know the man'" (v. 74). It's not a lie if you believe it, right? He has gone from sitting with the gospel's enemies to becoming one.

Then time speeds up: "Immediately a rooster crowed" (v. 75). Ah, Matthew. You've slowed time down in this last week of Jesus' life; that is, until this moment, when immediacy and urgency appear at just the right time. It happens precisely as Jesus predicted in verse 34, one more proof that he is firmly in control of events that seem to be spiraling out of control.

Peter remembers Jesus' prediction, comes to grips with the enormity of his betrayal, and Matthew reports, "And he went outside and wept bitterly" (v. 75). It's a haunting yet appropriate ending to this masterful scene.

Through it all, it shows us the honesty and vulnerability of the early church. Matthew knows it because Peter tells it. No doubt people respected Peter's leadership in those early days because he was open about his flaws, his failures, and his faith in redemption. Leadership wasn't about projecting an image; it was instead about proclaiming the truth, the messy truth about us and the glorious truth about Jesus.

That's the kind of leader I'd want to follow. That's the type of leader I want to be.

> *Healthy leaders don't project an image;*
> *they proclaim the truth.*

Day Eighty-Three
Matthew 27:1-10

Matthew skillfully weaves the story of Judas in with the story of Peter. Matthew follows Judas's betrayal with Peter's denial and then follows that with Judas's suicide. Laying their stories side by side in this way makes us ponder: What's the difference between the two? Why does the story of the one end in bloody tragedy, while the other ends in sacrificial triumph? Why do people name their sons Peter but no one names a child Judas?

Today's section begins with a time stamp: "Early in the morning" (27:1). Where did Jesus sleep? How late did last night's *trial* go? Matthew withholds those details from us. What we do know is that the religious elite (the chief priests and elders of the people) are eager to get on with the business of execution. Notice the verbs of verse 2: they "bound," "led," and "handed." Why did they have to present him to "Pilate the governor"? As an occupied people, the Jews did not have authority to enact capital punishment. They could find Jesus guilty, but they could not sentence him to death. They'd need the occupying force of Rome to do that. It's one case where they wanted to eliminate any separation between synagogue and state.

Then Matthew turns his attention to Judas: "When Judas, who had betrayed him, saw that Jesus was condemned, he was seized with remorse and returned the thirty pieces of silver to the chief priests and the elders" (v. 3). Why the remorse? The most likely explanation is that Judas expected his betrayal and Jesus' subsequent arrest to motivate Jesus to become a conquering Messiah who would then lead a military rebellion against Rome. In this light, then, his betrayal stemmed from his frustration that Jesus was not more revolutionary against the powers oppressing his people. When he saw that Jesus allowed himself to be arrested, tried, convicted, and condemned, he realized that his plans for the Savior's glory had gone sadly awry.

Judas attempted to redeem himself by returning the money: "I have sinned," he said, "for I have betrayed innocent blood" (v. 4). Who heard him say this? Matthew himself? The rest of the disciples? What would those conversations have been like? Again, our text is silent on these very interesting matters! The religious elite refused the repayment; Judas threw the money into the temple, and then "went away and hanged himself" (v. 5).

What if Judas's greater sin was believing that he couldn't be forgiven? What if viewing yourself as beyond Jesus' reach is actually worse than betraying him in the first place?

See you tomorrow as Jesus appears before Pilate, a character who, like Judas, is worthy of deep examination.

Your worst failure is no match for God's great love.

Day Eighty-Four
Matthew 27:11-26

....

Betrayal, darkness, deception, and even suicide have hovered over all the events of Thursday night. Our last image of Peter is alone with his failure and his tears. Surprisingly, we won't hear from him again in Matthew's Gospel. All the attention focuses on Jesus and how he perfectly executes his own execution.

The next scenes happen early on what we now know as Good Friday, as 27:1 has already made clear: "Early in the morning . . ." Over today's fifteen verses you'll read about negotiations between "the chief priests and the elders of the people" (27:1) and Pontius Pilate. Why is that? Why the back-and-forth between the Jewish religious elite and this Roman governor?

Here is the answer: Jerusalem was occupied territory. It was home to the Jews but governed by the Romans. One of the practical outcomes of that arrangement was that the Jewish leaders could not carry out capital punishment. They could sentence someone to death but were not empowered to carry it out legally. So the religious elite needed Rome's permission for and participation in an execution, especially an execution for the crime of blasphemy.

That charge is why Pilate is perplexed throughout the scene. He doesn't really understand, or care about, the crimes that Jesus has allegedly committed. So he asks this prisoner, "Are you the king of the Jews?" (v. 11a) and Jesus answers in the affirmative, sort of: "You have said so" (v. 11b). Then the accusations pile up, as does Jesus' refusal to answer them, and the result is "the great amazement of the governor" (v. 14), just like all the crowds at his miracles and teaching! Matthew uses the same word here that he does in describing public response to the feeding of the five thousand, the teaching of the parables, and the healings of those who are demon-possessed. The implication is that Jesus is here demonstrating his power by refusing to assert it. That may be the greatest miracle of all.

And then this: "Now it was the governor's custom at the festival to release a prisoner chosen by the crowd. At that time they had a well-known prisoner whose name was Jesus Barabbas" (vv. 15–16). So, as part of the Passover Festival, one prisoner per year gets "passed over" for punishment and is released. No bail needed! Orange jumpsuit comes off, civilian clothes returned, and freedom received. Notice that Pilate is aware of the motivations of the religious leaders: "For he knew it was out of self-interest that they had handed Jesus over to him" (v. 18).

Then the ultimate loyalty test for any married man: "While Pilate was sitting on the judge's seat, his wife sent him this message, 'Don't have anything to do with that innocent man, for I have suffered a great deal today in a dream because of him'" (v. 19). How is Matthew privy to this private exchange between the governor and the first lady? How does she know Jesus is innocent? We don't know the answers to those questions. What we *do* know is that Matthew carefully notes that Pilates receives the message while sitting in the judge's seat, a place of supreme authority. I have to believe Matthew is having fun here; Pilate *looks* like he has the authority, but his wife's note suggests a different reality altogether. She is more in control than Pilate, and Jesus is more in control than all of them.

As influential as Mrs. Pilate may be, the crowd is more so: "But the chief priests and the elders persuaded the crowd to ask for Barabbas and to have Jesus executed" (v. 20).

"What shall I do, then, with Jesus who is called the Messiah?" (v. 22). Notice how Pilate deflects responsibility: "who is called the Messiah." It's not my business; it's yours. What is implicit in these words becomes explicit in verse 24: "It is your responsibility!"

The answer chills: "Crucify him!"(v. 22). Say it again, louder this time: "But they shouted all the louder, 'Crucify him!'" (v. 23).

Remember the entrance into Jerusalem on the back of a colt? When Jesus received loud Hosannas? Matthew wants you to know that this crowd contains many of the same people; people who in the space of five days go from exalting Jesus to executing him. Why? Oh, many reasons—peer pressure, crowd dynamics, popularity—but at the heart of it all is something I have mentioned in sermons: there is something deep within the heart of humanity that hates the things of God. True then and true now. In demonstration of that fact, the crowd and the religious elite leading it gladly welcome ownership of the bloodguilt for Jesus' death: "His blood is on us and on our children!" (v. 25).

In the meantime, Barabbas becomes, in a literal fashion, the man in whose place Jesus died. Jesus becomes the substitute, enduring the punishment Barabbas deserves.

Barabbas is the first for whom that is true. But glory to God, not the last.

Jesus is the substitute for all of us who trust him to take the punishment we deserve.

Day Eighty-Five
Matthew 27:27-44

We're headed now into the bleakest part of the story. Yet in the masterful way Matthew weaves his narrative together, we do well to remember that we the readers are most horrified when Jesus the Savior is most glorified. We'll also see the many ways that, true to the form he established from the opening words of the Gospel, Matthew ensures this part of the story revolves around Jesus' identity.

First I want you to notice something about the verbs in today's section. The action moves from the religious—the chief priests, elders, and teachers of the law in 27:11–26—to the civic, as now it is "the governor's soldiers" (v. 17) who dominate the action. The Jewish leaders could sentence Jesus to death for blasphemy, but they had to have the Roman government actually carry out the execution. Those were the laws of occupation.

Focus on the verbs in verses 27–31. Note all the action of which Jesus is on the receiving end:

- The soldiers took (v. 27).

- They gathered a crowd (v. 27).

- They stripped him (v. 28).

- They put a scarlet robe on him (v. 28).

- They twisted and set [a crown of thorns] on him (v. 29).

- They put a staff in his right hand (v. 29).

- They knelt in front of him (v. 29).

- They mocked him (v. 29).

- They spat on him (v. 30).

- They struck him again and again (v. 30).

- They took off his robe and put his own clothes back on him (v. 31).

- They led him away (v. 31).

And then the culmination: to crucify him (v. 31).

Jesus is on the receiving end of mockery, brutality, and humiliation. Why does Matthew go to such lengths to portray Jesus as powerless here? As a recipient of scorn rather than a deliverer of salvation? Great questions! Yet questions that bring us back to the pattern that's been established ever since Jesus and his entourage first set foot in Jerusalem; he is in charge of every step, from locating the colt to securing the upper room to arranging for his own arrest. Even here, on the way to the cross, he is perfectly executing his own execution.

Notice one other feature of that opening paragraph from verse 29: "'Hail, king of the Jews!'" Jesus' identity has been Matthew's driving force throughout this Gospel: "What kind of man is this?" the disciples ask in 8:27. Well, the soldiers don't know it, of course, but their identification is 100 percent correct, as Jesus is, in fact, the king of the Jews and of everyone else who has ever lived.

The chaos and mockery continue in 27:32–44. A visitor in Jerusalem named Simon from Cyrene, a man Mark tells us is "the father of Alexander and Rufus" (Mark 15:21), is forced into the grisly duty of cross carrying. Why does Mark mention his two sons? Here's why: many students of Scripture believe that young Rufus grew up to be a leader in the Roman church, which is why Paul says "Greet Rufus, chosen in the Lord, and his mother, who has been a mother to me, too" (Rom. 16:13). Imagine the attention Rufus received when this

Gospel was read aloud in the Roman church and he received this cross-centered shout-out!

For all the buildup to the crucifixion, Matthew's actual description is remarkably spare: "When they had crucified him" (Matt. 27:35). His brevity, of course, is the source of his brilliance.

Jesus' identity returns as focus in verse 37, as the Romans not only call him the King of the Jews but make it semipermanent with a written notice on the cross itself: THIS IS JESUS, THE KING OF THE JEWS. Again, what man means for mockery, God turns into majesty.

We're horrified; Jesus is glorified.

The insults continue while Jesus endures the unique agony and humiliation built into crucifixion. He receives it from the crowd (v. 39), from the religious leaders (v. 41), and even from those crucified alongside (v. 44). Will anyone see through this gruesome scene for what it really is? Will anyone move from mocking him to worshiping him? Will anyone notice the glory that's being revealed through Jesus' suffering and humanity's wickedness?

*****

**What the world means for mockery,
God turns to majesty.**

*****

Day Eighty-Six
Matthew 27:45-56

....

Yesterday's reading included the briefest of descriptions: "[they] crucified him" (v. 35). Today we get a bit more detail, all of it rich with meaning, and some of it answering the question that has propelled the entire book.

Matthew is a master of what I would call *atmospherics*. With only a few words, he captures the scene in such a way the reader feels it. The scene at Golgotha is filled with both agony and darkness. Look at verse 45: "From noon until three in the afternoon darkness came over all the land."

Then there's verse 46, where Jesus utters the precise words that begin Psalm 22: "About three in the afternoon Jesus cried out in a loud voice, *'Eli, Eli, lema sabachthani?'* (which means 'My God, my God, why have you forsaken me?')." Jesus quotes it from the original Hebrew, speaking it in Aramaic, a Hebrew-related language he and his followers likely shared, Matthew writes it in Greek, the language of the New Testament, and we're reading it in English. Yet the Holy Spirit guided all that speaking, quoting, translating, and sharing. The implication of Jesus' "cry of dereliction" is clear. On the cross, he feels the utter absence of God. Bearing the weight of human sin (which we learn more clearly from Paul in places like 2 Cor. 5:16–21) and enduring the wrath of God, he experiences loss, lack, and loneliness. I have long suspected that by feeling the absence of God, Jesus encountered hell on earth so that we don't have to endure it after earth. Whatever else hell is, and New Testament imagery ranges from fire to darkness to a combustible garbage pit, it is at its core the absence of God. It's a mind-bending yet soul-saving thought: God the Son orchestrates a situation in which he experiences the utter absence of God the Father, and God the Holy Spirit inspires Matthew to capture its essence on the pages of our Scripture. What a Savior we have.

At the moment of death, Matthew tells us simply, "And when Jesus had cried out again in a loud voice, he gave up his spirit" (v. 50). His spirit wasn't taken from him; he gave it up. It's a subtle yet unmistakable way of affirming that Jesus is in control even in this moment of death.

Matthew 27:51–53 has inspired no little conjecture through the centuries: "At that moment the curtain of the temple was torn in two from top to bottom. The earth shook, the rocks split and the tombs broke open. The bodies of many holy people who had died were raised to life. They came out of the tombs after Jesus' resurrection and went into the holy city and appeared to many people." What is Matthew's purpose in including this event?

Of all those questions, that final one—Matthew's purpose—is the most important. Does he wish to wow us with a special-effects story that didn't happen in history but impresses us literarily? Or did these events really happen, as strange as they may be?

On those questions, it's helpful to remember Matthew's tone and his language. His tone in this small narrative is matter-of-fact, even if the tale he tells is bewildering. The way he tells this story strongly suggests he wants us to take it as fact. Second, his language makes clear that God is the main actor in this unlikely turn of events. Note, for example, the passive voice in the verbs as the curtain "was torn" (v. 51), the tombs "broke open" (v. 52a), and the bodies "were raised to life" (v. 52b). The passive voice suggests an outside actor and the miraculous nature of what occurred implies that outside actor is the Lord.

Who exactly was raised, and how long did they stay living? Matthew declines to give us a definite answer, though the fact that their "bodies" (v. 52) were raised at least somewhat intact raises the possibility that they were more the recently dead of Jerusalem than the patriarchs that Genesis describes. Ultimately, whatever happened was to prepare us for an even more miraculous and more enduring resurrection coming three days later, in Matthew 28.

What if, however, an even more significant though less spectacular miracle takes place just one verse after a city full of walking dead people? Read Matthew 27:54: "When the centurion and those with him who were guarding Jesus saw the earthquake and all that had happened, they were terrified, and exclaimed, 'Surely he was the Son of God!'" Now, why is that identification so miraculous?

What is a question that drives Matthew? "What kind of man is this?" (8:27) This Gospel is an identity narrative in which the readers know from the outset what the characters do not: that Jesus is Messiah, the Son of the living God. Early in the book, only the demons make this identification. Then at one of the book's great turning points in Matthew 16:16, Peter becomes the first human being to declare "You are the Messiah!" He has trouble understanding what kind of Messiah Jesus will be, but his identification is momentous nonetheless. Now at the foot of the cross, a Roman soldier—a Gentile and an outsider—sees the manner in which Jesus dies and says, "Surely he was the Son of God!" First the spirit world. Then the Jewish inner circle. Now the Gentile observers. This is not only how the realization dawns; this is how the Gospel spreads—"[first] in Jerusalem, and [then] in all Judea and Samaria, and [then] to the ends of the earth" (Acts 1:8). If you know what Matthew has been doing from the beginning, you realize just how sublime this moment becomes. Your own spiritual ancestry is in some way linked back to this *outsider*, who is not circumcised, not kosher, not a "chosen person," and who declares faith in Israel's Messiah. Again, Matthew is genius and Jesus is glorious.

Jesus is dead. What will his followers do with his body? What precautions will his adversaries take so that no rumors will spread regarding his afterlife? How will the Romans and the religious elite conspire to make sure there is no Matthew 28?

Recall the first time you acknowledged that Jesus truly is the Son of God. What kind of strength or even euphoria did that realization bring you? That's a memory you can't revisit too often.

Day Eighty-Seven
Matthew 27:57-65

....

When we left off yesterday's reading, Jesus had "[given] up his spirit" in verse 50 (it wasn't taken from him). A Roman soldier began the expansion of the gospel by acknowledging that Jesus is the Son of God, and several women continued to offer support while the men headed for the hills in fear.

It was common for the Romans to leave a criminal's body on the cross for multiple days, allowing scavenging animals to have their fill while signaling to the masses: this is your fate if you oppose us. It was chilling, gruesome, and very effective.

Jewish custom from Deuteronomy 21:22–23 was to bury the body as quickly as possible. That explains Matthew 27:57–58: "As evening approached, there came a rich man from Arimathea, named Joseph, who had himself become a disciple of Jesus. Going to Pilate, he asked for Jesus' body, and Pilate ordered that it be given to him." We know from Luke that Joseph was a member of the Sanhedrin, so by identifying with Jesus in this public yet sensitive way, he was no doubt hurting his own standing in the community. Notice the extensive details Matthew gives us regarding this burial in verses 59–60:

He took the body.

He wrapped it in a clean linen cloth.

He placed it in his own tomb.

He rolled a big stone in front of it.

He went away.

As with the other books in the Bible, Matthew was designed to be read out loud. I feel sure the earliest public readers placed special, percussive emphasis on all those verbs, and along the way ensured that Joseph would never be forgotten.

Matthew 27:61 gives us one more reminder as to the identity of the story's heroes: "Mary Magdalene and the other Mary were sitting there opposite the tomb." Matthew throws shade at himself and the other male disciples. They are not even in the story at this saddest of moments!

In the next scene (vv. 62–66), we see the ultimately futile attempt by the Jews and Romans to keep Jesus dead and to stop any rumors from being born. It's a desperate, evil alliance between synagogue and state. The chief priests approach Pilate "after Preparation Day," which most experts believe implies that they did it on the Sabbath (v. 62). In other words, they were so eager to stop the Jesus Movement that they would break one of their own most sacred Sabbath laws. Notice how they describe Jesus in verse 63: "that deceiver," a name typically reserved for Satan. They assert that if any resurrection story spreads, "this last deception will be worse than the first" (v. 64c).

Pilate complies with the request by assigning a guard, securing the tomb, and placing a seal on the tomb (vv. 65–66). What was that seal? Likely made of wax or clay, it served to authenticate that the person behind it was truly dead. If the seal was broken, it would be evidence of grave tampering. If you have checked into a hotel recently (in this post-COVID era), you have seen seals across the door, a signal that the room is COVID-Clean. Open the door, break the seal, and the room is yours. That's much the role of this seal over Jesus' tomb.

Everything has been made ready to squash the Jesus Movement and to prevent it from getting started. The plan between the Jews and the Romans is thorough, meticulous, and foolproof.

The attempt is ultimately doomed to failure. If people had been compelled to faith by how Jesus died, imagine their response when they learn the grave was just a temporary residence, borrowed for three days.

God turns Satan's weapons of destruction into tools for deliverance.

Day Eighty-Eight
Matthew 28:1-10

M atthew 27 concluded with the plot to protect the tomb belonging to Joseph of Arimathea and containing Jesus. Matthew 28 begins with the epic failure of that foolish plan.

Matthew is careful to let us know yet again that the women around Jesus remain courageous while the men are so cowardly they are absent: "After the Sabbath, at dawn on the first day of the week, Mary Magdalene and the other Mary went to look at the tomb" (28:1).

Our inspired author fills the next verses (2–3) with vivid language and decisive verbs: "There was a violent earthquake, for an angel of the Lord came down from heaven and, going to the tomb, rolled back the stone and sat on it. His appearance was like lightning, and his clothes were white as snow."

Those last two descriptors make us think immediately of Jesus' own transfiguration in Matthew 17. Is this what everyone in glory looks like, whether redeemed people or angelic messengers?

The guards, so central to the Roman-Jewish plot to prevent resurrection from happening, "shook and became like dead men" (v. 4). These men will assume center stage in tomorrow's reading. Their "like dead men" implies two things: First, their abject fear of what they have witnessed. Second, their fear that the Romans will execute them for their failure to prevent an earthquake, an angel, and a resurrection!

The angel's voice and demeanor appear calm in light of the violence, noise, and light of this most unusual of mornings: "The angel said to the women, 'Do not be afraid, for I know that you are looking for Jesus, who was crucified" (v. 5). Then the angel has the privilege of announcing the greatest victory in the history of the universe: "He is not here; he has risen, just as he said" (v. 6).

With that announcement, the universe shifts, the world tilts, and nothing is the same again. Note how, yet again, the Bible is understated where we'd be **ALL CAPS AND BOLDED WITH MANY EXCLAMATION MARKS!!!!**

Perhaps the matter-of-fact tone of the angel comes from his realization that resurrection comes with an assignment containing two imperatives: Come and see (v. 6); Go and tell (v. 7).

Come and see. Go and tell. See what Jesus has done. Then tell others. Experience. Proclaim. Live it. Share it. God offers rescue and redemption but does so with the demand that we not hoard the good news but spread it instead.

In case we miss the thrust of this first resurrection scene, Matthew repeats the command, this time from the mouth of Jesus. As the women obey what the angel has told them to do, they encounter Jesus himself. Unlike John's account, where Mary mistakes him for the gardener, here his identity is clear: "Suddenly Jesus met them" (v. 9). By the way, don't be alarmed that the four Gospel accounts don't harmonize perfectly; that shows us the events they're describing defy human logic and that they didn't collude in crafting their stories.

When Jesus meets the women, he repeats the command: "Do not be afraid. Go and tell my brothers to go to Galilee; there they will see me" (v. 10). Absent men need courageous women to tell them about the risen Jesus. In other words, the first preachers of the gospel are female, and the first requirement of resurrection is proclamation.

With whom will you share that news today? Whom will you tell?

Of all the great religious figures in human history, Jesus is the only one who claimed to be God and then proved it by rising from the dead. You can't say that often enough.

Day Eighty-Nine
Matthew 28:11-15

....

This brief section is unique to Matthew, as none of the other Gospels record it in their post-resurrection narratives. By including it, Matthew brings the desperation of Jesus' civil and religious opponents to an absurd conclusion.

It begins with the subtlest of reminders of exactly who are the human heroes of Jesus' last days on earth: "While the women were on their way . . ." (v. 11a). The women were "on their way" from the tomb to begin Gospel Proclamation. Where are the men? Peter, James, John, Matthew, and the rest? Hiding in fear for their lives! Is it not clear that God's work will prevail, whether he has to work in spite of us or alongside of us?

While the women were acting heroically, "some of the guards went into the city and reported to the chief priests everything that had happened" (v. 11b). If the guards were Roman soldiers, as seems likely, I find it interesting that they went first to the Jewish leaders. Perhaps they felt that if they went directly to Pilate and his cronies, their punishment would be immediate and lethal. In any event, the chief priests then met with the elders and "devised a plan [to give] the soldiers a large sum of money, telling them, 'You are to say, "His disciples came during the night and stole him away while we were asleep."'" (vv. 12–13).

For the soldiers, the motivation for the plan is clear from verse 14: "If this report gets to the governor, we will satisfy him and keep you out of trouble." For the Jewish leaders, the motivation is more simple: to quell the Jesus Movement before it can even begin. Matthew wants his original audience to know the fruit of his investigative reporting, for "this story has been widely circulated among the Jews to this very day" (v. 15).

Ponder for a moment the lengths to which the Hebrew-Roman alliance has gone to eliminate Jesus:

- bribery to Judas in order to arrange the betrayal

- a sham trial that violated many of their own religious laws

- slander to bring him before Pilate

- cowardice and manipulation to stir up the crowd to get the answer they wanted: "Give us Barabbas; crucify Jesus!"

- bribery (again) to silence the truth of the resurrection

And at every level, the plan failed. Miserably.

Think about it from this perspective. In the earliest days after that first Easter, all the Hebrew-Roman alliance would have had to do to stop the church in its tracks was to produce Jesus' dead corpse, place it in the center of Jerusalem's marketplace, and declare, "Here is your risen Savior." But they didn't because they couldn't. They didn't because they couldn't.

How will a Gospel that begins with a trip through Jesus' family graveyard come to a conclusion? What will a story dominated by the many words of Jesus do for its encore?

From the beginning, the powers that be have tried to quell the Jesus Movement. It didn't work then, and it won't work now.

Day Ninety
Matthew 28:16-20

....

We started this eighty-nine days ago. As we conclude Matthew's Gospel, I want to refresh your mind with how it begins and what has been its emphasis. Matthew begins with a trip through Jesus' family graveyard, his genealogy. That genealogy itself begins with Abraham, the first man of the covenant and the father of the Jewish people. From opening words, then, Matthew has sought to demonstrate to his largely Jewish readership that Jesus is the fulfillment of everything that is Israel. He is the greater Abraham, the better Moses, and the completion of God's work with the chosen people that began so long ago.

With that in mind, Jesus' closing words stun us with their global perspective. Previously in Matthew's resurrection scenes, Jesus has appeared to the women (because the men are nowhere to be found) and has been the subject of a denial plot by the Hebrew-Roman alliance.

All that is mere prelude to the final scene. Look how it starts: "Then the eleven disciples went to Galilee, to the mountain where Jesus had told them to go" (v. 16). Both the resurrection messenger in verse 7 and Jesus himself in verse 10 had given word to be shared with the remaining disciples: go to Galilee. This, apparently, is a command they can obey! Matthew must note with sadness that there are now only eleven of them, as Judas the betrayer has already met his Maker.

I have read this scene many times but never noticed the subtle detail of verse 17: "When they saw him, they worshiped him; but some doubted." "But some doubted." Huh. Is that Thomas, whose story John tells in much more detail? Or is it Thomas plus some others? What did they doubt? Why? How did Jesus deal with their doubts? Of those questions, we only know the answer to the last one: Jesus dealt with their doubts by giving them an assignment, which we read in verses 18–20. There has to be some greater principle here, as in "if you really want to overcome your doubts, get to work." Perhaps: "Don't wallow in doubt; work it out." Or even, as I've said before, "Doubt justifies disobedience, but surrender magnifies understanding."

In the church world we call this *the Great Commission*. If you think about it closely, it is the reason every single one of you who is a Christian today first heard about Jesus. Let me show you what I mean.

The Great Commission is rooted in the Savior's identity: "All authority in heaven and on earth has been given to me" (v. 18). Whatever follows from Jesus' mouth flows from that reality. He doesn't share the throne with anyone. He is not a prime minister who can be voted out; he is the King who will one day come to claim his own. His authority is comprehensive and complete. It is futile to resist it.

What happens from that authority? "Therefore, go and make disciples of all nations, baptizing them in the name of the Father and of the Son and of the Holy Spirit" (v. 19). This verse forms the heart of the commission.

Go. Don't wait; don't stay; don't even beckon them to come to you. Go. It's why the book of Acts details the expansion of the church throughout the known world of the Mediterranean basin. It's why Paul took so many missionary journeys. It's why missionaries through the centuries have taken the gospel to lands where it has not been heard. And get this (and this is thrilling): it's why, today, missionaries from the developing world in the Global South are coming to North America! They've heard how our culture resists and resents the gospel, and so they're sending pastors and teachers and tentmakers to turn us back around.

"Make disciples." Not "make converts." Not "make attenders." Not "make fans." Make *disciples*, people who follow the Rabbi Jesus so closely that they begin to resemble him in attitude and action alike. Guess what? I believe your commitment to and nourishment from your time in Matthew and through this guide is one of the primary ways you're becoming a *disciple* rather than merely an *attender*. Another way of phrasing the word *disciple*? A living relationship with Jesus Christ. Aha!

Next it says "of all nations" (v. 19). In the original language, that term *nations* refers more to people groups than it does to modern nation-states. In the single nation-state of India, for example, there are literally hundreds of different people groups. Those are the objects of Jesus' affection and the church's mission. Jesus has already suggested that when such gospel saturation happens, "then the end will come" (24:14). At the congregation I serve, Good Shepherd Church in Charlotte, North Carolina, we have a remarkably strategic location in which many people groups flood to our area naturally. On one Sunday, for an example, you can hear an Indian pray in the Oriya dialect, an Angolan pray in Portuguese, a Texan preach in English, a Puerto Rican testify in Spanish, and musicians of all colors and backgrounds lead us along the way. That's just in one local church; imagine what God does in places of greater diversity and deeper impact!

Notice what Jesus, in Matthew's hands, has done in verses 18–19. A gospel that begins with a Jewish emphasis concludes with a firmly Gentile target. A movement that starts *local* goes *global*. Jesus' story launches from the "bosom of Abraham" to the ends of the earth. Remember how I've said that in Jesus we find the fulfillment of the Jewish people and mission? Matthew 28:19 hearkens back to the original call of Abraham in Genesis 12:3: "I will bless those who bless you, and whoever curses you I will curse; and all peoples on earth will be blessed through you."

Now we know how and through whom that happens.

Jesus' finals words promise us the power to make it happen: "And surely I am with you always, to the very end of the age" (v. 20). The Great Commission is so vast, so urgent, and so comprehensive that there's no way we could do it in our own power. Thank God we don't have to.

Jesus' closing words open up the world.